GW01454506

Fidel Castro. Beyond the Cuban Revolution. Biography

MARKO D

ISBN:9798320977362

Table of Contents

Acknowledgments

As I embark on the journey of narrating the life of Fidel Castro, a figure both admired and reviled, I am reminded of the complexities and contradictions that define human history. Castro, a name that echoes through the annals of modern history, is a character who cannot be understood through a monochrome lens. His story, woven into the very fabric of the 20th century, is as intricate as it is impactful.

First, I extend my gratitude to the historians and biographers who have previously charted the course of Castro's life. Their diligent work laid the foundations I could build, offering a mosaic of perspectives that challenge and enrich my understanding. Their dedication to preserving history, with its inherent biases and subjectivities, reminds them of the responsibility of narrating the past.

I must also thank those who lived through the Castro era, whose personal stories and anecdotes breathe life into the pages of history. In their recollections, we find the hues of humanity, often lost in the grand narrative. These personal narratives, whether of admiration, fear, or disillusionment, are crucial in painting a holistic picture of Castro's Cuba.

I owe a debt of gratitude to the people of Cuba, both on the island and in the diaspora. Their resilience and spirit, amidst the tumultuous waves of their nation's history, provide an indispensable context. Their diverse and rich experiences serve as a testament to the indomitable human spirit that persists in the face of hardship and change.

Special thanks go to the scholars and experts in Cuban history, politics, and culture who generously shared their insights. Their expertise was invaluable in navigating the complex socio-political landscape in which Castro's story is set. Their critical perspectives challenged my assumptions and guided my understanding of the intricate web of global politics and local dynamics.

I am also grateful to the translators and interpreters of Spanish and Cuban dialects, whose skill in language bridged the gap between cultures and times. Their work allowed me to access primary sources and oral histories that would have otherwise remained beyond reach, adding depth and authenticity to this biography.

My editorial team deserves a heartfelt acknowledgment. Their keen eyes and sharp minds have been instrumental in shaping this narrative. Their patience, perseverance, and commitment to accuracy and clarity have supported this extensive endeavor.

Finally, I extend my deepest appreciation to you, the reader. Your interest in understanding the multifaceted narrative of Fidel Castro's life is not just a curiosity but a powerful contribution to our collective quest for knowledge and truth. It is for you that these pages were written, with the hope that they offer not just information, but a portal to a time and place that have significantly shaped our world.

In writing this biography, I have walked through the corridors of history alongside a man who was both a revolutionary hero and a controversial dictator. This journey, fraught with the complexities of human nature and the vagaries of political power, has been enlightening. Through these pages, you, too, will experience the multifaceted saga of Fidel Castro, a figure who not only shaped the destiny of a nation but also left an indelible mark on global politics.

A Prologue to Inspiration

Have you ever wondered what forces shape a leader? What intricate blend of history, circumstance, and personality forges a figure like Fidel Castro, whose name is etched in modern history? This is not just the story of a man but of an era, a revolution, and a small Caribbean island that captured the world's imagination.

Fidel Castro. The mere mention of his name evokes many images: a bearded revolutionary in olive green, a charismatic speaker, and a global figure in the Cold War era. But who was he, indeed? Castro's life is a tapestry of fascinating contradictions and enigmas. His transformation from a young law student to the leader of a guerrilla movement and eventually to the enduring face of Cuban communism is a narrative that borders on the unbelievable.

But let's not rush. To truly grasp Castro, we must delve into the details, the lesser-known aspects of his life that molded him. His formative years, characterized by a relatively privileged upbringing and an education oscillating between traditional Catholic schools and progressive ideologies, laid the groundwork for a multifaceted personality. Was it these early influences that ignited the spark of revolution in Castro? Or was it something deeper, something inherent in the spirit of this young Cuban?

As we explore Castro's life, we encounter a series of pivotal moments: the failed Moncada Barracks attack, his imprisonment, the daring journey on the Granma yacht, and the grueling guerrilla warfare in the Sierra Maestra mountains. Each event is a thread in the fabric of Castro's rise to power. But what about the man himself? What about his personality, his dreams, his fears? How did he perceive his role in the world, and how did the world, in turn, perceive him?

This biography is not a mere chronicle of Castro's life; it's an endeavor to fathom the man behind the public image. How did he retain power for so long in a world where leaders rise and fall? What ideologies and convictions propelled him? And, importantly, what was his vision for Cuba, and how did this vision reshape the lives of millions of Cubans?

Castro's impact on the world stage cannot be overstated. From the Cuban Missile Crisis, which brought the world to the brink of nuclear war, to his role in shaping the Non-Aligned Movement, his actions had global repercussions. His alliances with the Soviet Union and his defiance of the United States challenged the established world order. But at what cost? And to what end?

We must also examine Castro's legacy, which remains a subject of intense debate. To some, he is a hero, a symbol of resistance against imperialism, and a champion of social justice. To others, he is a tyrant, an oppressor who stifled freedom of expression and led his country into economic ruin. This biography seeks to navigate these contrasting views, not to judge, but to present a balanced view of a deeply complex individual.

As we embark on this journey through Castro's life, I invite you to keep an open mind. Let's try to understand the man, not just the leader. Let's explore what he did and why he did it. And remember, history is not just about events and dates; it's about people – flesh and blood, with dreams and fears, strengths and weaknesses.

So, where do we start? At the beginning, of course. Let's turn back the pages to a young Fidel in the rural landscapes of Birán, embarking on a path that would lead him to become one of the most iconic figures of the 20th century. Welcome to the story of Fidel Castro, which is as captivating as it is controversial...

Chapter 1

Childhood in Birán

In the lush landscapes of eastern Cuba, nestled among sugarcane fields and towering palm trees, lies Birán, a small town that cradled the early years of Fidel Castro. Imagine a young Fidel running barefoot, his laughter mingling with the rustling leaves and chirping birds. This is where our story begins, in the heart of rural Cuba, where the seeds of revolution were unwittingly sown.

Born on August 13, 1926, to Ángel Castro, a prosperous sugarcane farmer, and Lina Ruz González, Fidel was the third of seven children. His father, an immigrant from Spain, had worked tirelessly to amass wealth. This feat provided Fidel with a childhood of relative privilege. Yet, despite the comfort, young Fidel's life was not insulated from the realities of Cuban society, marked by stark inequalities and simmering unrest.

Fidel's early years blended rural simplicity and complex familial dynamics. His strict disciplinarian father was often away, managing the family's extensive landholdings. In his absence, Fidel's mother, Lina, became the nurturing force, instilling in him the values of empathy and justice. Could these early experiences have sparked the flame of rebellion in Fidel? Did the contrast between his family's affluence and the poverty of the local laborers shape his future ideology?

Education played a pivotal role in young Fidel's life. Initially homeschooled, he was later sent to Santiago de Cuba and Havana for formal schooling. His years at La Salle and Dolores School and later at Belén Jesuit Preparatory School exposed him to various ideas and philosophies. Here, amidst the rigors of a Catholic education, Fidel began to develop a keen sense of social justice. The young Castro was not just a student of textbooks; he was a student of life, absorbing the disparities and injustices that plagued his country.

But Birán was always calling him back. The memories of his childhood, playing in the fields and listening to the stories of the laborers, remained etched in his mind. It juxtaposed worlds: the lush green fields and the harsh realities of those who toiled on them. Did this dichotomy plant the seeds of dissent in Fidel's mind? How did a child, born into relative comfort, grow to challenge the foundations of Cuban society?

The answer, perhaps, lies in the very essence of Birán. It was more than just a physical space; it was a microcosm of Cuba, reflecting the island's broader social and economic disparities. For young Fidel, Birán was both a playground and a classroom, where his character was molded and his worldview shaped.

In these early chapters of Fidel's life, we see glimpses of the man he would become. The restless energy of a child who refused to be confined by the norms, the sharp intellect of a student who questioned the status quo, and the emerging leader who would one day steer the course of his nation's history. Birán was not just a place; it was the beginning of a journey that would lead Fidel Castro from the sugarcane fields of eastern Cuba to the global stage.

As we delve deeper into Fidel Castro's life, we carry with us the image of a young boy in Birán who looked at the world around him and dared to dream of change. This is where it all started, in the heart of Cuba, in the small town of Birán.

Education and Early Influences

In the landscape of Fidel Castro's life, his education and early influences are crucial pillars that shaped the man he would become. Picture a young Fidel, his mind as fertile as the Cuban soil, absorbing the myriad lessons that would later forge the leader of a revolution. This part of his journey is about the schools he attended and the crucible of ideas and experiences that molded his early worldview.

Castro's educational journey began in the rustic setting of Birán. Still, it was in Santiago de Cuba, at the La Salle boarding school, where his formal education took root. Can you imagine the young boy, accustomed to the freedoms of rural life, now adapting to the discipline of a Catholic institution? Here, among the sons of Cuba's elite, Fidel first encountered the stark disparities of wealth and poverty. These early years were not just about learning to read and write; they were about reading the world and writing his perceptions of it.

The transition to Belén Jesuit Preparatory School in Havana significantly shifted Castro's life. At Belén, a renowned educational institution, Fidel was exposed to a rigorous curriculum and an ethos emphasizing social justice, as taught by the Jesuits. This environment, coupled with the intellectual ferment of Havana, provided a fertile ground for the young Castro. His teachers, steeped in liberation theology, played a pivotal role in shaping his social and political views. Was it here, in the classrooms and corridors of Belén, that the seeds of rebellion were sown in Castro's mind?

However, Castro's education was not confined to the walls of schools. The vibrant streets of Havana, teeming with political discourse and the rumblings of discontent against the Batista regime, were equally instructive. Fidel's forays into university politics at the University of Havana were more than just a young man's quest for identity; they were a baptism into the fiery world of activism. The university became a microcosm of the national struggle, and Castro quickly made his mark with his burgeoning leadership qualities and a keen sense of justice.

Amidst the rigors of academic life, Fidel found his calling in the political ferment of the times. He absorbed the writings of Cuban nationalists like José Martí and international figures like Marx and Lenin, whose ideas on socialism and class struggle resonated with him. But it wasn't just the written word that influenced Castro. The suffering of the Cuban people under the dictatorship, the stories of inequality and injustice, the spirit of resistance – these were the lessons that no classroom could impart. They were the lessons learned on the streets, in the struggles of the ordinary people.

Fidel's early life was a confluence of influences — the disciplined environment of Jesuit education, the university's political awakening, the injustices he witnessed firsthand, and the rich tapestry of Cuban culture. Each played its part in shaping his ideology and identity. But how did these elements converge to create the leader of a revolution? What was it about these early years that set Castro on a path that would alter the course of Cuban history?

As we delve deeper into Fidel Castro's life, these questions linger. His education and early influences provide a window into the making of a revolutionary, offering glimpses into the complex interplay of personal experiences and broader historical forces. In understanding these formative years, we begin to unravel Castro's enigma, a man who would become both a symbol of resistance and a figure of controversy in world history.

Political Awakening

Fidel Castro's journey into the heart of political activism is a narrative of transformation and awakening. It's a story not just of a young man coming to terms with his political beliefs but of an emerging leader who would one day shake the very foundations of Cuban society. This chapter of Castro's life is an intricate tapestry woven with threads of intellectual curiosity, patriotic enthusiasm, and an unyielding sense of justice.

Castro's political awakening began to take a definitive shape during his years at the University of Havana. Was the 1940s a tumultuous era for Cuba, marked by political instability and social unrest? The university, a hotbed of political thought and debate, became the crucible where Castro's ideological views were forged. Fidel found his voice amid the vibrant discussions and passionate arguments. But what drove this young student to embrace such a radical path?

It was a combination of factors: the pervasive corruption within the Cuban government, the growing influence of American businesses on the island's economy, and the stark inequalities that blighted Cuban society. These were not just abstract issues for Castro; they were tangible, visceral realities he witnessed daily. The suffering of the Cuban people, the exploitation of the workers, the suppression of dissent – these were the sparks that ignited the fire of rebellion in him.

As Castro immersed himself in the political scene at the university, he became increasingly influenced by the ideologies of anti-imperialism and nationalism. The writings of José Martí, the Cuban national hero, particularly resonated with him. Martí's vision of a free and independent Cuba, unshackled from foreign domination, became a guiding principle for Castro. But how did this young law student, who once harbored ambitions of a legal career, become the face of a revolutionary movement?

The answer lies in Castro's inherent leadership qualities and ability to connect with the masses. He had a charismatic presence, an oratorical prowess that could captivate audiences, and a profound conviction in his beliefs. These attributes were evident in his early forays into student politics, where he championed the cause of social justice and national sovereignty. Fidel's activism was not limited to the confines of the university; he actively participated in protests and campaigns against the government's policies, earning him both admiration and notoriety.

However, Castro's political awakening was not just about fiery speeches and street protests. It was also a period of intellectual maturation. He delved deeply into Marxist-Leninist literature, absorbing the theories of class struggle and the proletariat's role in shaping history. These ideas profoundly influenced his understanding of Cuba's predicaments and envisioned solutions.

One cannot overlook the influence of global events on Castro's political evolution. The Spanish Civil War, the rise of fascism in Europe, and the emerging Cold War provided a broader context for his ideological development. These events reinforced his belief in the need for radical change in Cuba and globally. Castro's political awakening was not an insular process but inextricably linked to the broader currents of world history.

As we trace the contours of Fidel Castro's political awakening, we see the emergence of a complex figure: a man deeply committed to his ideals, unafraid to challenge authority, and determined to alter the course of his nation's history. This period of his life is pivotal, for it lays the foundation for his future actions. In understanding this phase, we begin comprehending the motivations and aspirations of one of the 20th century's most enigmatic leaders.

Castro's journey from a young, dynamic student to the architect of a revolution is a testament to the power of conviction and the indomitable spirit of resistance. It's a story of how ideas can take root and grow, how a single individual's awakening can become a collective call to action. In Fidel Castro's political awakening, we find the genesis of a leader who would leave an indelible mark on Cuba and the world.

Chapter 2

Moncada Barracks: The First Battle

The story of Fidel Castro can only be told by pausing at the Moncada Barracks, the site of his first significant battle. This foray would mark both a beginning and a symbolic moment in his life. This episode, fraught with audacity and youthful zeal, set the stage for the narrative that would define not just Castro's life but the future of an entire nation.

It was July 26, 1953. The air was thick with tension and anticipation as Castro, then a young, impassively audacious lawyer, led an assault on the Moncada Barracks in Santiago de Cuba. Why did Castro choose to launch an attack on one of the largest military garrisons in Cuba? The answer lies in a mix of strategic calculation and symbolic gesture. Castro aimed to spark a nationwide uprising against the corrupt and dictatorial regime of Fulgencio Batista, who had seized power in a military coup. Moncada was not just a military target but a statement, a declaration of intent against tyranny.

But the assault did not go as planned. Imagine the chaos, the confusion, and the sound of gunfire echoing through the barracks. The rebels, though determined, were outnumbered and outgunned. The aftermath was brutal: many of Castro's comrades were killed, and he, along with others, was captured. This moment of defeat, however, did not signify the end.

Instead, it became a pivotal turning point in Castro's life and the Cuban revolution.

Castro's trial following the failed assault was a spectacle in itself. Defiant and unbroken, he turned the courtroom into a platform for his ideology. His speech, later published as "History Will Absolve Me," was a masterful blend of personal defense and political manifesto. In it, Castro outlined his vision for Cuba: a nation free from tyranny, rooted in social justice, and sovereign in its affairs. The young lawyer's eloquence and conviction were remarkable in the face of certain convictions. He famously declared, "Condemn me; it does not matter. History will absolve me."

Castro was sentenced to 15 years in prison in the Isle of Pines. But even behind bars, his influence continued to grow. How did this young man, now a political prisoner, manage to keep the spirit of rebellion alive? Castro's prison resilience and ability to inspire and organize his fellow inmates only added to his growing legend. His time in prison was a period of reflection and strategizing, solidifying his views and planning for the future.

The failed Moncada assault and Castro's subsequent imprisonment became rallying points for opposition to Batista's regime. They sparked a movement that would eventually lead to a full-scale revolution. In a twist of fate, under political pressure and public outcry, Batista released Castro and his fellow revolutionaries as part of a general amnesty in 1955. This release set the stage for the next chapter in Castro's life and the Cuban revolution.

The Moncada Barracks assault was, in many ways, a microcosm of Castro's revolutionary journey. It embodied his audacity, unwavering belief in his cause, and ability to turn setbacks into sources of strength. This event encapsulated the beginning of Fidel Castro's transformation from a rebellious young lawyer into a revolutionary icon.

Imprisonment and Ideological Evolution

These years behind bars were not a period of stagnation for Castro but a crucible for his ideological evolution and political maturation. In his cell's confinement, future revolutionary strategies and philosophies were sown.

Castro's imprisonment began in 1953 following the unfortunate attack on Moncada Barracks. Sentenced to 15 years in the Isle of Pines Prison, he found himself in an environment far removed from the tumultuous streets of Havana. Yet, this change in setting did not dampen his spirit; instead, it gave him a rare opportunity for introspection and deep study. How did Castro use this time to evolve from a rebellious figure into a visionary leader?

During his imprisonment, Castro immersed himself in a rigorous study of history, politics, and economics. He devoured books, delving into the works of Marx, Lenin, and Martí. These texts were not just reading material for Castro; they were the tools that helped him refine his ideology and craft his vision for Cuba. In the silence of his cell, away from the outside world's distractions, Castro began to piece together a coherent philosophy that combined nationalist fervor with socialist principles. But how did these intellectual pursuits translate into practical strategies for his future revolutionary activities?

One of the critical aspects of Castro's time in prison was his ability to maintain and strengthen his leadership role among his fellow revolutionaries. Despite the constraints of imprisonment, he continued to communicate with his comrades, exchanging ideas and planning for the future. Castro's charisma and conviction turned his cell into a classroom where discussions on revolutionary strategy and Cuban history were common. These interactions kept the spirit of rebellion alive and helped forge a tighter bond among the revolutionaries.

Castro's ideological evolution during his imprisonment was also marked by a growing awareness of the need for broad-based support for his revolutionary goals. He recognized that overthrowing Batista's regime would require more than just a small group of armed rebels; it would need the backing of the Cuban people. This realization led him to envision a more inclusive movement that addressed the wider population's aspirations and concerns. How did this shift in perspective influence his subsequent approach to revolution?

Another significant aspect of Castro's imprisonment was the development of his thoughts on guerrilla warfare. Inspired by the writings of Mao Zedong and other revolutionary theorists, Castro began to contemplate the role of guerrilla tactics in the Cuban context. He understood that traditional warfare methods would be futile in the face of a superior military force. Thus, his strategies began to favor the idea of a protracted guerrilla war. This plan would later prove instrumental in his quest for power.

Castro's release from prison in 1955, as part of a general amnesty, marked the end of a crucial chapter in his life. He emerged from prison not as a defeated rebel but as a renewed revolutionary, equipped with a clearer ideological vision and a strategic blueprint for the liberation of Cuba. His confinement was a significant transformation, laying the intellectual and strategic groundwork for the revolution.

Castro's imprisonment was a paradoxical blessing. It was a time of isolation that fostered connectivity, a period of restriction that broadened his ideological horizons, and a moment of apparent defeat that set the stage for his ultimate triumph. In the narrative of Fidel Castro's life, the years of imprisonment stand as a testament to the power of resilience and the capacity of the human spirit to evolve and adapt in the face of adversity.

History Will Absolve Me

Spoken in the wake of his capture after the Moncada Barracks assault in 1953, these words were not merely a defense in court; they were a manifesto, a vision, and a prophecy. This speech, delivered under the most dire of circumstances, encapsulated the essence of Castro's ideology and his steadfast commitment to the Cuban revolution.

Castro, then a young lawyer, found himself in a courtroom, not as an attorney but as a defendant, accused of organizing an armed uprising against the Batista regime. However, Fidel Castro, ever the orator, turned the tables. The courtroom became his stage, the audience not just judges but the Cuban people, and history itself. But what was it about this speech that made it so iconic?

Firstly, it was the context. Castro delivered "History Will Absolve Me" when Cuba was reeling under the oppressive rule of Fulgencio Batista. The nation cried out for change, and Castro's words echoed this collective yearning. He began by justifying the Moncada attack not as a bid for power but as a necessary step against tyranny. Castro's eloquence transformed his trial into a public indictment of Batista's government, highlighting the corruption, brutality, and illegitimacy of the regime.

But "History Will Absolve Me" was more than just an indictment of Batista; it was a blueprint for a new Cuba. In his speech, Castro laid out his vision for the nation – agrarian reform, industrialization, restoration of civil liberties, and education for all. These were not just lofty ideals but tangible goals underpinned by a deep understanding of Cuba's socio-economic landscape. Castro's words painted a just, sovereign Cuba, free from foreign domination and social inequality.

This speech also marked a pivotal moment in Castro's personal journey. In these moments, standing before a court, Castro fully embraced his role as a revolutionary leader. His words transcended the individual, touching the hearts and minds of countless Cubans. "History Will Absolve Me" was a rallying cry, a call to arms, and a declaration of hope. Castro's unwavering belief in the righteousness of his cause resonated most profoundly.

Moreover, "History Will Absolve Me" was prophetic. With remarkable foresight, Castro declared that even if the court condemned him, history would vindicate him. This statement was not just an act of defiance but a deep conviction in the inevitable triumph of justice over tyranny. Castro's confidence in the historical inevitability of revolution was bold and incredibly audacious, considering his circumstances.

The legacy of "History Will Absolve Me" is enduring. Historians, revolutionaries, and political theorists have celebrated, analyzed, and critiqued it. The speech did not just defend a political action; it defined a political era. Its repercussions were felt far beyond the courtroom, inspiring not only Cubans but people across the globe fighting against oppression.

"History Will Absolve Me" is a testament to Fidel Castro's rhetorical prowess, political acumen, and unshakeable belief in the Cuban revolution. These words, spoken in the early stages of his political career, encapsulated the spirit of defiance and hope that would characterize his entire life. In this speech, Castro laid the foundation for his legacy, which remains as complex and contested as the man himself.

Chapter 3

Forming the 26th of July Movement

The formation of the 26th of July Movement marks a defining moment in Fidel Castro's journey and the history of Cuba. This movement, named after the date of the Moncada Barracks assault, became the embodiment of Castro's revolutionary ideals and the vehicle through which he would eventually reshape Cuba's destiny.

Castro was in a radically different political landscape after his release from prison in 1955 under a political amnesty. The Moncada attack had failed but ignited a national conversation about resistance against the Batista regime. However, the question lingered: How could this momentum be transformed into a structured movement capable of toppling a well-entrenched dictatorship?

Castro, ever the strategist, realized that a new approach was needed. The 26th of July Movement was his answer to this challenge. But what was this movement all about, and how did Castro envision it functioning? Fundamentally, it was a revolutionary organization aimed at overthrowing Batista and establishing a democratic, socially progressive government. But it was also more than that; it symbolized hope and resistance for the Cuban people, who were weary of corruption and oppression.

In the formative days of the movement, Castro focused on building a cohesive group of loyal and dedicated revolutionaries. He reached out to those who had participated in the Moncada assault, students, intellectuals, and workers disillusioned with the Batista regime. It was a diverse group but united by a common goal – the liberation of Cuba. How did Castro galvanize such a varied group into a unified force?

One of Castro's key strengths was his charismatic leadership and ability to articulate a vision resonating with the masses. He spoke of social justice, land reform, restoring civil liberties, and national sovereignty. These were not just abstract concepts; they were concrete issues that affected the everyday lives of Cubans. Castro's rhetoric was potent, blending nationalism with a call for social change, and it struck a chord with many who longed for a better future.

However, forming the movement was just the first step. The real challenge was organizing it into an effective force. Castro and his fellow leaders set about creating a network of cells across Cuba. These cells operated clandestinely, organizing protests, spreading propaganda, and recruiting new members. The movement also sought support from exiles and sympathizers abroad, particularly in Mexico and the United States. But how did Castro keep the movement cohesive and focused, given the inherent risks and challenges of operating under a repressive regime?

The answer lay in Castro's discipline and strict code of conduct. Despite the movement's decentralized nature, decisions were often centralized, with Castro himself overseeing major strategies. This centralized command, coupled with the decentralized execution, allowed the movement to be flexible and responsive to the rapidly changing political landscape.

Another significant aspect of the movement was its commitment to armed struggle. Castro believed that only a sustained guerrilla campaign could bring down Batista. His study of guerrilla warfare shaped this belief and the lessons learned from the Moncada assault. The movement, therefore, began to train and arm its members, preparing for the eventual armed insurrection.

Under Castro's leadership, the 26th of July Movement quickly grew in size and influence. It became a symbol of defiance against tyranny, capturing the imagination of Cubans from all walks of life. The movement's green and black armbands became a visible sign of resistance, worn proudly by those who dared to dream of a free Cuba.

In the story of Fidel Castro and the Cuban revolution, the formation of the 26th of July Movement stands as a critical chapter. It was the crucible where Castro's revolutionary ideals were tempered and tested. More than just a political organization, it was the birth of a movement that would change the course of Cuban history. The legacy of the 26th of July Movement, with its bold aspirations and relentless pursuit of justice, remains a pivotal moment in a nation's struggle for freedom and dignity.

The Sierra Maestra Campaign

The Sierra Maestra campaign is a testament to Fidel Castro's resilience and tactical genius, marking a pivotal chapter in his ascent as a revolutionary leader. This campaign, a series of guerrilla operations conducted in the rugged Sierra Maestra mountains of eastern Cuba, was not just a military endeavor; it was a crucial phase in transforming the 26th of July Movement into a formidable force capable of challenging the Batista regime.

The story of the Sierra Maestra campaign begins in late 1956, after Castro's strategic regrouping in Mexico. Along with 81 other revolutionaries, including the iconic figures Che Guevara and Camilo Cienfuegos, Castro embarked on the audacious mission aboard the yacht Granma. This perilous journey culminated in their arrival in Cuba but was fraught with challenges right from the start. The group faced immediate setbacks, including an ambush by Batista's forces shortly after landing, which scattered the revolutionaries and significantly reduced their numbers. How did Castro, with a handful of survivors, manage to regroup and launch a successful guerrilla campaign?

The answer lies in Castro's unwavering determination and ability to adapt to the most challenging circumstances. The Sierra Maestra mountains provided the perfect terrain for guerrilla warfare, with its dense forests and rugged terrain offering natural cover. Castro and his band of revolutionaries began to wage a war of attrition against Batista's troops. However, what made the Sierra Maestra campaign truly remarkable was not just the guerrilla tactics but also the way

Castro leveraged this period to build a parallel political strategy.

Amidst the harsh conditions and constant threat of enemy attacks, Castro focused on winning the hearts and minds of the rural population. He understood that the success of his movement hinged on popular support. Thus, the Sierra Maestra campaign was as much about engaging with the local peasants, addressing their grievances, and spreading the revolutionary ideology as it was about military engagements. Castro's natural charisma and policies that favored agrarian reform and social justice helped garner significant peasant support. But how did this grassroots support translate into a strategic advantage?

The increasing support from the rural populace provided crucial intelligence, resources, and recruits for Castro's growing army. It allowed the movement to expand operations, carrying out more frequent and effective attacks against government forces. The guerrillas, now seasoned by the rigors of mountain warfare and bolstered by growing ranks, began to pose a severe threat to Batista's army.

Another significant aspect of the Sierra Maestra campaign was its impact on national and international perceptions. Castro's ability to survive and even thrive in the Sierra Maestra, against all odds, added to his legend. During this time, significant publications, including American newspapers, began to cover his struggle, bringing international attention to the Cuban revolution. But how did this media attention affect the movement?

The international spotlight helped shape a narrative of a romantic and righteous struggle against an oppressive regime. It drew global sympathy and support, bolstering the movement's morale and legitimacy. Moreover, it put additional pressure on the Batista regime, which was already struggling to maintain its grip on power.

The Sierra Maestra campaign, which lasted from 1956 to 1958, was not just a series of military victories; it saw Castro evolve from a rebel leader to a symbol of revolutionary zeal. It demonstrated his strategic acumen, his ability to inspire loyalty and his knack for propaganda. This campaign laid the groundwork for the final push toward Havana and, ultimately, the triumph of the Cuban revolution.

In the larger narrative of Fidel Castro's life, the Sierra Maestra campaign emerges as a crucial turning point. In the rugged mountains of Cuba, Castro's vision of revolution took a tangible form, setting the stage for the dramatic events that would follow and forever change the course of Cuban history.

Strategy and Solidarity

Strategy and solidarity play central roles, intertwining in his journey from a rebel leader to the head of a transformative revolution. Castro's strategic understanding, combined with his ability to foster a deep sense of solidarity among his followers, was fundamental to the success of the Cuban revolution.

Castro demonstrated a keen understanding of military and political strategy from his revolutionary activities. His approach was not one of brute force but of calculated moves designed to maximize impact with limited resources. But how did he develop these strategies that would eventually topple a well-entrenched regime?

One key element of Castro's strategy was his focus on guerrilla warfare. Drawing inspiration from Mao Zedong's and Che Guevara's works, Castro realized that traditional military tactics were unsuitable against Batista's superior forces. Instead, he adopted a guerrilla approach, emphasizing mobility, flexibility, and the element of surprise. This strategy turned the rebels' weaknesses into strengths, allowing small, agile units to damage government forces significantly.

However, Castro's strategic brilliance was not confined to the battlefield. He was acutely aware of the importance of the political dimension in his struggle. He worked tirelessly to build a broad coalition of support, reaching out to peasants, workers, students, and even middle-class Cubans. But how did he manage to unite such a diverse array of groups under a common cause?

The answer lies in his ability to foster a sense of solidarity among his followers. Castro's speeches and writings consistently emphasized themes of national pride, social justice, and anti-imperialism. He painted the revolution as a collective struggle for a better future, not just for the privileged few but for all Cubans. This message resonated deeply with a populace weary of Batista's corruption and inequality.

Solidarity was also built through shared hardships and sacrifices. The rebels' time in the Sierra Maestra mountains was marked by complex conditions and constant danger. These experiences created strong bonds among the fighters, with Castro often leading by example. His willingness to share in the hardships endured by his men boosted morale and fostered a sense of camaraderie.

Moreover, Castro's strategy extended beyond Cuba's borders. He was adept at garnering international support, using the media to draw attention to his cause. His interviews with foreign journalists helped shape global perceptions of the Cuban revolution, presenting it as a legitimate and moral struggle against tyranny. This international solidarity was crucial in providing ethical and material support to the movement.

However, Castro's approach was not without its critics. Some within the movement disagreed with his centralized decision-making and insistence on absolute loyalty. Yet, even among these dissenting voices, there was a recognition of Castro's leadership qualities and his unwavering commitment to the revolution.

Strategy and solidarity were the twin pillars upon which Castro built his revolutionary project. His strategic insights enabled him to navigate the complex landscape of Cuban politics and warfare. At the same time, his ability to inspire solidarity gave him the support base necessary to challenge an entrenched regime. These elements were not just tactics but reflections of Castro's deep understanding of power dynamics and human motivation. Few have managed to blend these elements in the history of revolutionary movements as effectively as Fidel Castro did in his quest to transform Cuba.

Chapter 4

Gaining Popular Support

Fidel Castro's ascent as a revolutionary leader and the eventual success of the Cuban revolution were significantly bolstered by his remarkable ability to gain and maintain popular support. This aspect of his journey reveals not just his political savvy but also his deep understanding of the Cuban psyche and the prevailing socio-economic conditions of the time.

At the heart of Castro's strategy for gaining popular support was his keen awareness of the Cuban people's aspirations and grievances. The Batista regime, characterized by corruption, repression, and subservience to foreign interests, had created widespread discontent among various segments of society. With his charismatic persona and eloquent oratory, Castro tapped into this reservoir of discontent, channeling it into a powerful force for change.

But how exactly did Castro convert this general sense of dissatisfaction into a concrete support base for his revolutionary agenda? One key factor was his ability to articulate a vision of Cuba that resonated with a broad spectrum of the population. He spoke of social justice, agrarian reform, national sovereignty, and restoring democratic freedoms. These were not just abstract ideals; they addressed the everyday concerns and struggles of the Cuban people, from the urban working class to the rural peasantry.

Castro's approach to building popular support was multifaceted. In urban areas, his movement engaged in propaganda campaigns, organized demonstrations, and fostered alliances with labor unions and student groups. In the countryside, particularly in the Sierra Maestra mountains, Castro and his guerrillas worked to win the trust and support of the rural peasantry. They implemented agrarian reforms, redistributed land, and provided healthcare and education. Often overlooked in conventional military strategies, these actions were crucial in building a grassroots support base.

Moreover, Castro's charisma played a significant role in winning hearts and minds. He was often seen as a man of the people, someone who, despite his relatively privileged background, understood and shared the struggles of the average Cuban. His willingness to live and fight alongside his men, endure the same hardships, and risk his life for the cause earned him not just respect but a deep and enduring loyalty.

Another significant aspect of Castro's strategy was his adept use of media and propaganda. He was acutely aware of radio, print, and, later, television's power in shaping public opinion. His interviews with foreign journalists and broadcasts on Radio Rebelde effectively informed the Cuban populace and gained international sympathy for his cause. These efforts helped to counteract the negative propaganda disseminated by the Batista government, presenting the July 26 Movement as a legitimate and moral effort to reclaim Cuba for its people.

Castro's ability to gain popular support was also a testament to his political acumen in navigating the complex landscape of Cuban politics. He managed to maintain a delicate balance, appealing to both moderate and radical elements within Cuban society. His promises of land reform and social justice appealed to the left. At the same time, his nationalist rhetoric and commitment to restoring constitutional rule resonated with more conservative segments.

Gaining popular support was a critical element in Castro's journey to power. His success in this regard was due to a combination of strategic vision, charismatic leadership, a deep understanding of the Cuban context, and effective communication and propaganda. This support was instrumental in sustaining the revolution during the struggle against Batista and in the consolidation of power that followed. Castro's ability to connect with the Cuban people and mobilize them in pursuit of a common goal remains one of the most significant aspects of his legacy.

Key Battles and Tactical Shifts

In the saga of Fidel Castro's revolutionary struggle, the key battles and tactical shifts play pivotal roles, epitomizing his strategic understanding and ability to adapt to changing circumstances. These engagements and maneuvers shaped the course of the Cuban Revolution. They solidified Castro's reputation as a resilient and ingenious military leader.

The journey of the July 26 Movement under Castro's command was marked by several critical battles that were both symbolic and strategic in nature. These confrontations were not mere military engagements; they were the crucibles where the revolution's fate was forged.

One of the earliest and most significant battles was the attack on the Moncada Barracks in 1953. Although this assault ended in failure and led to Castro's imprisonment, it was pivotal in rallying widespread support for the revolutionary cause. The boldness of the attack and the subsequent trial and imprisonment of Castro and his fellow revolutionaries ignited a national discourse on the need for change in Cuba.

After his release and exile to Mexico, Castro underwent a period of tactical reevaluation. He recognized the need for a different approach and shifted his focus toward guerrilla warfare. This change in strategy was influenced by his study of insurgent movements worldwide and the unique topography of Cuba, which favored guerrilla tactics.

The Granma Expedition of 1956 marked the beginning of this new phase. Although the landing was disastrous, with most of the expedition members either killed or captured, Castro, along with a small group including Che Guevara and Raúl Castro, managed to escape to the Sierra Maestra mountains. It was here that Castro's prowess in guerrilla warfare began to shine. The dense and rugged terrain provided a natural advantage, allowing Castro's small force to launch hit-and-run attacks against Batista's forces, gradually gaining strength and recruits.

The Battle of La Plata in 1958 was one of the first significant victories for Castro's guerrilla army. This battle demonstrated the effectiveness of his guerrilla tactics and boosted the morale of his forces. It also showed Castro's ability to orchestrate complex military operations with limited resources.

Another significant engagement was the Battle of Las Mercedes. In this encounter, Castro skillfully negotiated a ceasefire, which he used to reorganize and strengthen his forces, showcasing his tactical ingenuity. This move was a turning point, leading to a series of victories that increased pressure on Batista's army.

Throughout these campaigns, Castro's leadership was characterized by flexibility and adaptability. He was quick to modify his tactics in response to the changing dynamics on the battlefield and the needs of his growing army. His ability to maintain high morale among his troops and his skill in propaganda further solidified his position as a leader.

Castro's strategies extended beyond the battlefield. He understood the importance of international support and effectively used the media to garner sympathy for his cause. His interviews with foreign journalists and broadcasts on Radio Rebelde played a crucial role in shaping international opinion favoring the revolution.

In the final stages of the revolution, Castro's forces implemented a general offensive, moving out of the Sierra Maestra and launching attacks in other parts of Cuba. This expansion of operations signaled a shift from guerrilla warfare to conventional warfare, as his forces were now strong enough to engage Batista's army in open combat.

The capture of Santa Clara in December 1958, led by Che Guevara, was one of the final blows to the Batista regime. This victory, achieved through guerrilla tactics and conventional warfare, paved the way for Castro's triumphant entry into Havana and marked the end of Batista's rule.

The key battles and tactical shifts in Castro's revolutionary campaign were instrumental in his rise to power. These events highlight his strategic foresight, adaptability, and leadership qualities. They also underscore the importance of understanding the socio-political context and leveraging military and non-military assets in a revolutionary struggle. Castro's journey from the Moncada Barracks to Havana is not just a tale of military conquest but a testament to the power of strategic thinking and resilience in the face of adversity.

The Fall of Havana

The fall of Havana in January 1959 marked a pivotal moment in Fidel Castro's revolutionary campaign. This historic event symbolized the end of Fulgencio Batista's regime and heralded a new era for Cuba. This crucial moment in Castro's life story was the culmination of years of struggle, strategy, and resilience, and it represented a significant shift in the political landscape of Latin America.

In the twilight hours of December 31, 1958, as the world celebrated the dawn of a new year, Batista, facing inevitable defeat, fled Cuba. His departure resulted from a series of strategic victories by Castro's forces, steadily gaining ground across the island. The fall of Havana, however, was not just the result of military triumphs; it was a victory shaped by the changing tides of public opinion and the collapse of the regime's support domestically and internationally.

As Castro prepared to enter Havana, the atmosphere in Cuba was electric with anticipation. The streets, once scenes of strife and conflict, were now swarming with jubilant crowds eagerly awaiting the rebels' arrival. But how did Castro, once a young law student, lead his band of guerrillas to this momentous victory?

Castro's journey to Havana was a masterclass in guerrilla warfare and revolutionary strategy. From the rugged Sierra Maestra mountains to the urban centers of Cuba, his campaign was marked by astute military tactics and a deep understanding of Cuba's socio-political landscape. His ability to mobilize widespread support, not just from his fighters but also peasants, workers, and the urban middle class, was instrumental in eroding the foundations of Batista's power.

Upon entering Havana, Castro was not just taking control of a city but assuming the mantle of national leadership. The immense challenges ahead tempered the jubilation and relief that greeted him. Castro was now responsible for steering Cuba towards a new future that he had envisioned as a fairer, more just society.

The fall of Havana also marked a significant ideological shift in the region. It was a moment that resonated far beyond Cuba's borders, inspiring leftist movements across Latin America and the world. Castro's victory was seen as a beacon of hope for those fighting against oppression and imperialism, and it positioned Cuba at the forefront of the global Cold War dynamics.

However, the takeover of Havana also set the stage for the transformative and often controversial changes that Castro would implement. His policies, ranging from agrarian reform to nationalizing industries and establishing a one-party state, would not only reshape Cuban society but also redefine its relationship with the United States and the Soviet Union.

The fall of Havana is not just a testament to Castro's leadership and the resolve of his followers; it is a chapter in a larger story of a nation's quest for sovereignty and identity. It marked the end of an era of dictatorial rule in Cuba and the beginning of a complex and challenging journey toward a new social and political order.

As historians and observers analyze Castro's life and legacy, the fall of Havana remains a defining moment, encapsulating the triumphs and tribulations of a revolution that continues to evoke debate and discussion. This event was not merely the conclusion of a military campaign; it was the start of a profound transformation of Cuban society, with Fidel Castro at its helm.

Chapter 5

Initial Reforms and Policies

The advent of Fidel Castro's leadership in Cuba was marked by a flurry of reforms and policies to radically transform the nation's socio-economic landscape. These initial reforms, introduced soon after Castro's rise to power in 1959, were driven by his commitment to social justice and his vision of a socialist Cuba. This period of Castro's life was characterized by vigorous activity as he sought to address the inequalities and grievances that had fueled the Cuban Revolution.

One of Castro's first and most significant reforms was agrarian reform. For decades, Cuba's agricultural sector was dominated by large estates, many of which were owned by foreign companies. Most rural workers lived in poverty, with little to no land to call their own. Castro's government moved swiftly to dismantle this system. The Agrarian Reform Law, enacted in May 1959, aimed to redistribute land among peasant farmers and nationalize estates larger than a specific size. This radical policy was a decisive step towards altering the structure of Cuba's economy and empowering the rural poor. But how did this reform impact the broader socio-economic fabric of Cuba?

Land redistribution was more than just an economic measure; it was a symbolic gesture that underscored the revolution's commitment to the marginalized. It fostered a sense of ownership and participation among the peasantry, who could cultivate their land for the first time. However, this reform also had its challenges, including inefficiencies and resistance from those who had lost their landholdings.

Another critical area of reform was education. Before the revolution, literacy rates in Cuba were low, and access to education was limited, especially in rural areas. Castro, who believed strongly in education as a tool for empowerment and development, initiated a nationwide literacy campaign. Teachers and students were mobilized across the island to teach reading and writing, dramatically increasing literacy rates within a year. This campaign was not just about literacy; it was a profound transformation of the educational landscape, making education accessible to all segments of society.

Castro also focused on healthcare reform. The new government implemented policies to provide free medical care to all citizens, establishing rural clinics and hospitals, and training more doctors. These efforts significantly improved health standards and made Cuba a public health model in the developing world.

In addition to these social reforms, Castro's government began nationalizing foreign-owned businesses and properties, particularly those of American companies. This move was part of a broader strategy to gain control over the nation's resources and reduce foreign influence in Cuba's affairs. However, these nationalizations led to deteriorating relations with the United States, culminating in the imposition of a trade embargo that would have long-lasting effects on Cuba's economy.

Furthermore, Castro's initial policies also included efforts to reduce unemployment and raise wages. These measures were popular among the working class but strained the Cuban economy. Managing the economic impacts while trying to fulfill the revolution's social goals became a significant challenge for Castro's government.

The initial years of Castro's rule were a time of radical change and optimism for many Cubans. The sweeping reforms and policies introduced during this period reflected Castro's desire to create a more equitable society aligned with socialist ideals. However, these changes were also met with controversy and resistance, both domestically and internationally, setting the stage for the complex and often contentious path that the Cuban Revolution would follow in the coming years.

Fidel Castro's initial reforms and policies set into motion a transformative agenda that would reshape Cuba in profound ways. They reflected his revolutionary ideals and the challenges of implementing widespread change in a society marked by deep inequalities and external pressures. These early years of Castro's rule were pivotal in defining his legacy and the future of Cuba, encapsulating the hopes, struggles, and complexities of a nation in transition.

Navigating Global Politics

Fidel Castro's ascent to power and subsequent rule over Cuba cannot be fully understood without delving into his navigation of global politics. His leadership unfolded during intense Cold War tensions, where international politics were predominantly characterized by the rivalry between the United States and the Soviet Union. Castro's Cuba was at the heart of this geopolitical maelstrom, with its leader skilfully maneuvering between the superpowers.

Castro's foray into global politics was as audacious as his domestic policies. Initially, after the 1959 revolution, Cuba's relations with the United States were cautious but not overtly hostile. However, the situation quickly deteriorated due to Castro's radical reforms, particularly the nationalization of industries, many of which were American-owned. The United States, viewing Castro's leftist leanings and close ties with communist countries as a threat in its backyard, responded with economic sanctions and diplomatic isolation. But how did Castro react to these measures?

In response to American hostility, Castro turned to the Soviet Union, marking a significant shift in Cuba's foreign policy. This alliance provided Cuba with much-needed economic and military support. However, aligning with the Soviet Union was risky and placed Cuba at the center of Cold War tensions. The most dramatic manifestation of this was the Cuban Missile Crisis of 1962. This 13-day standoff brought the world to the brink of nuclear war. Castro's role in the crisis was controversial; he advocated a hardline approach against the United States, further exacerbating tensions.

Despite the risks, Castro's alliance with the Soviet Union had several advantages. It provided a security umbrella that shielded Cuba from direct military aggression, and it ensured economic aid that was crucial for Cuba's survival given the U.S. embargo. Castro, leveraging his relationship with the Soviets, also sought to expand his influence in the global arena, particularly in the developing world.

Under Castro's leadership, Cuba became active in international politics, especially in Latin America and Africa. He supported leftist movements and governments, most notably in Angola and Nicaragua. Castro's commitment to anti-imperialism and his success in standing up to the United States made him a symbol of resistance and inspiration for many revolutionaries and leftist leaders across the globe.

However, Castro's navigation of global politics was not without its challenges and criticisms. His close ties with the Soviet Union were often seen as compromising Cuba's independence, making the island nation a pawn in the more giant Cold War game. Moreover, his support for revolutionary movements abroad sometimes backfired, straining Cuba's relations with other countries and diverting resources from domestic development.

The collapse of the Soviet Union in the early 1990s posed a significant challenge to Castro's regime. Cuba lost its most important ally and economic supporter, plunging the island into a severe financial crisis known as the "Special Period." Castro's response to this new reality was a mix of pragmatism and resilience. He implemented economic reforms to attract foreign investment. He opened up the tourism sector while maintaining tight control over the political system.

Castro's navigation of global politics was marked by a strategic balancing act. He maintained an anti-imperialist stance and alignment with socialist principles while adapting to changing global dynamics. His leadership during this period was characterized by ideological steadfastness and pragmatic flexibility, which kept Cuba relevant on the world stage despite its small size and limited resources.

Fidel Castro's legacy in international politics is complex and multifaceted. Many revere him as a champion of anti-imperialism and a defender of the Global South against the hegemony of superpowers. Others criticize him for his alignment with the Soviet Union and authoritarian governance style. Despite these differing views, Castro's impact on global politics during the Cold War era remains undeniable, marking him as one of the most influential and controversial figures in the 20th century's international relations.

The Bay of Pigs Invasion

The Bay of Pigs Invasion, a pivotal episode in the life of Fidel Castro and a defining moment in the Cold War era, stands as a testament to his leadership and the resilience of the Cuban revolutionary spirit. Occurring in April 1961, this failed military invasion, orchestrated by the United States, aimed to overthrow Castro's nascent revolutionary government. It not only dramatically altered Cuba's relationship with the U.S. but also solidified Castro's power and international standing.

The invasion was the culmination of mounting tensions between Cuba and the United States following Castro's rise to power. The U.S. government, alarmed by Castro's nationalization of American-owned industries and his increasingly close ties with the Soviet Union, approved a CIA plan to train and arm a group of Cuban exiles known as Brigade 2506. The plan was to invade Cuba and incite an uprising against Castro. But how did Castro repel this well-planned attack with his relatively small and inexperienced armed forces?

Castro, aware of the potential for an American-backed attempt to overthrow his government, had been preparing his forces for any such eventuality. His intelligence networks had been on high alert, and when the invasion finally came, he was not surprised. The invaders landed at the Bay of Pigs, a remote swampy area on Cuba's southern coast. This choice would prove to be a strategic blunder for the attackers.

Under Castro's direct command, the Cuban revolutionary forces responded with surprising speed and efficiency. Despite being outnumbered and outgunned, the Cuban militia, bolstered by Soviet-supplied weapons, showed remarkable resilience. Castro's leadership during the invasion was crucial. He not only directed military operations but also rallied the Cuban people, emphasizing the invasion as an imperialist aggression against Cuban sovereignty.

The U.S.-backed forces quickly found themselves trapped on the beach without sufficient support. The expected popular uprising against Castro did not materialize; instead, the Cuban populace broadly rallied to support their leader. Within 72 hours, the invasion was crushed, with many of the attackers killed or captured. The Bay of Pigs Invasion had failed, leaving the United States embarrassed internationally.

The aftermath of the invasion had far-reaching consequences. Domestically, it bolstered Castro's image as a nationalist hero who had successfully defended his country against the might of the United States. It also justified his tightening grip on power and further crackdowns on opposition. Internationally, it pushed Cuba closer to the Soviet Union, leading to increased military and economic support from the communist bloc.

For Castro, the Bay of Pigs Invasion was more than a military victory; it was a political triumph. It legitimized his rule in the eyes of many Cubans. It reinforced the revolutionary narrative of Cuba as a small island nation capable of resisting American imperialism. It also showed his capability as a strategist, anticipating enemy moves and responding effectively.

Moreover, the invasion had a significant impact on the Cold War dynamics. It deepened the rift between the United States and Cuba, setting the stage for further confrontations, most notably the Cuban Missile Crisis. It also heightened the sense of a global struggle between the capitalist West and the communist East, with Cuba becoming a symbol of resistance against Western domination in the developing world.

The Bay of Pigs Invasion is a critical chapter in Fidel Castro's biography. It showcases his leadership, strategic acumen, and ability to unite his people in the face of external threats. This event not only defined Castro's rule in the years to come but also left an indelible mark on the history of the Cold War and Latin American politics. The Bay of Pigs is a poignant reminder of the complexities of international relations and the enduring impact of small nations in the global geopolitical landscape.

Chapter 6

Aligning with the Soviet Union

Fidel Castro's alignment with the Soviet Union was a pivotal chapter in his biography and the broader narrative of the Cold War. This strategic alliance significantly shaped the trajectory of his regime and had profound implications for global politics. The Cuba-Soviet Union relationship, evolving from a pragmatic alignment to a profound ideological bond, played a central role in defining Castro's leadership and the fate of Cuba.

In the aftermath of the Cuban Revolution in 1959, Castro faced immense challenges, including significant hostility from the United States. The nationalization of American-owned businesses in Cuba had soured relations, leading to economic sanctions and diplomatic isolation by the U.S. In this context, the Soviet Union emerged as a natural ally for Castro. But what drove Castro, initially not a communist, to align with the Soviet bloc?

The primary factor was pragmatic: Cuba needed economic and military support to survive in the face of American hostility. The Soviet Union, keen on extending its influence in the Western Hemisphere, saw an opportunity in Castro's Cuba. They provided the island with crucial economic aid, military equipment, and technical assistance. This support was vital for Castro to consolidate his power and implement his social and economic reforms.

However, Castro's alignment with the Soviet Union was not merely a marriage of convenience but also ideologically driven. Over time, Castro's ideology had evolved to fully embrace Marxist-Leninist principles, and the relationship with the Soviet Union helped to solidify this ideological shift. Under Castro's leadership, Cuba adopted socialist policies, including the collectivization of agriculture and the centralization of industry. The Cuban government promoted socialist values and education, aligning the nation's social fabric closely with Soviet-style communism.

This alliance had its most dramatic manifestation during the Cuban Missile Crisis 1962. The Soviet Union, with Castro's consent, had placed nuclear missiles in Cuba aimed at the United States. This act dramatically escalated Cold War tensions, bringing the world to the brink of nuclear conflict. Castro's role in the crisis was controversial; he advocated for a strong stance against the United States, even at the risk of nuclear war. The crisis eventually ended with the Soviet Union withdrawing the missiles in exchange for U.S. concessions. The crisis resolution left Castro feeling betrayed by Soviet leader Nikita Khrushchev, exposing the complexities of the Cuba-Soviet relationship.

Despite these tensions, the Cuba-Soviet Union alliance remained strong until the collapse of the Soviet bloc in the early 1990s. The Soviet Union was Cuba's primary trading partner and source of aid. This support was crucial for Cuba's economy, which had become heavily dependent on Soviet subsidies. Cuban troops, supported by the Soviet Union, also participated in various Cold War conflicts, most notably in Angola and Ethiopia, showcasing Castro's commitment to supporting anti-imperialist movements globally.

The dissolution of the Soviet Union in 1991 had profound consequences for Cuba. The loss of economic support plunged the island into a severe financial crisis known as the "Special Period." Castro's regime faced its most significant challenge yet, struggling to find a new economic model and maintain social stability. The end of the Soviet Union also marked the end of an era for Castro; he was forced to navigate a post-Cold War world where Cuba's strategic significance had diminished.

Castro's alignment with the Soviet Union was a defining aspect of his leadership. It was a decision driven by economic necessity, ideological affinity, and geopolitical considerations. This alliance bolstered Castro's regime, enabling him to withstand American pressure and pursue his revolutionary goals. However, it also made Cuba heavily dependent on the Soviet bloc, a vulnerability that became starkly evident with the Soviet Union's collapse. The Cuba-Soviet relationship was complex, marked by mutual benefits, ideological solidarity, and strategic challenges. It remains a crucial part of understanding Fidel Castro's legacy and the dynamics of Cold War politics.

Nationalization and Agrarian Reform

Fidel Castro's rise to power in Cuba was quickly followed by sweeping economic changes, primarily through nationalization and agrarian reform. These reforms, deeply rooted in Castro's socialist ideals, aimed at redistributing wealth and reducing foreign influence in Cuba's economy. While these policies garnered support from specific population segments, they also led to significant international tension, particularly with the United States.

Nationalization, a cornerstone of Castro's economic policy, began in earnest in 1960. The Cuban government took control of foreign-owned businesses, particularly those owned by American companies. This move was driven by a desire to gain economic independence and to assert national sovereignty. Castro's government viewed the heavy American presence in Cuba's economy as a form of neocolonialism, perpetuating inequality and hindering the development of the country's resources for the benefit of its people. The nationalization policy was bold, signaling a clear break from Cuba's previous economic policies and its alignment with U.S. interests.

However, the nationalization drive had far-reaching consequences. It resulted in an immediate backlash from the United States, which saw its businesses and interests directly threatened. The U.S. responded with a trade embargo, severely impacting the Cuban economy. This embargo, which remains in place to this day, has been a constant source of economic hardship for Cuba and has shaped much of its subsequent economic policy.

Alongside nationalization, agrarian reform was another significant policy implemented by Castro. Before the revolution, Cuba's agricultural sector was dominated by large estates, often owned by foreign companies or wealthy individuals. Most rural workers lived in poverty, with little land to call their own. Castro's Agrarian Reform Law, introduced in 1959, aimed to change this. The law stipulated the expropriation of estates more extensive than a specific size and their redistribution to peasant farmers. This reform was not only economic but also social in nature, seeking to empower the rural poor and reduce income inequality.

The agrarian reform had a profound impact on Cuban society. It improved the living conditions of many peasants, giving them land and a stake in the country's future. However, it also faced significant challenges. Land redistribution led to decreased agricultural productivity, partly due to the new landowners' need for more experience and resources. Furthermore, the reforms alienated some sectors, including more affluent farmers who lost their land. They contributed to tensions with the United States, which saw its citizens' properties expropriated without compensation.

In Castro's vision, these reforms were essential to building a socialist society in Cuba. He believed that control of the nation's resources should be in the hands of the Cuban people, not foreign companies or a wealthy elite. These policies were part of a broader strategy to reduce inequality, increase self-sufficiency, and improve the standard of living for the average Cuban.

However, implementing nationalization and agrarian reform policies also had downsides. The alienation of the United States and other Western powers led to Cuba's increased economic and political reliance on the Soviet Union. This dependence became particularly problematic after the Soviet Union's collapse, leaving Cuba in a precarious financial situation.

The nationalization and agrarian reform policies implemented under Fidel Castro were transformative for Cuba. They reflected his commitment to socialist principles and desire to reduce foreign influence and economic inequality in Cuba. While these policies had some positive domestic impacts, they also contributed to significant challenges, both in terms of economic hardships resulting from the U.S. embargo and Cuba's eventual dependency on the Soviet bloc. These reforms were a defining feature of Castro's leadership and significant to his legacy.

Resistance and Repression

Fidel Castro's leadership in Cuba was marked by revolutionary change and social reforms, significant resistance, and subsequent repression. His tenure as Cuba's leader was a complex blend of achieving social goals and maintaining a tight grip on power, often leading to harsh measures against dissent and opposition.

From the earliest days of the Cuban Revolution, Castro faced resistance from various quarters. This resistance came from the remnants of the Batista regime and those who opposed his increasingly authoritarian methods and alignment with the Soviet Union. There were also those within Cuba who opposed the implementation of rapid social and economic changes.

To address this resistance, Castro's government established mechanisms of control and repression. The Committees for the Defense of the Revolution (CDR), formed in 1960, served as neighborhood watchdogs, reporting on counter-revolutionary activities and promoting social welfare. While the CDRs played a role in mobilizing the population for health campaigns and other social initiatives, they also monitored dissent, contributing to an atmosphere where dissent could be seen as disloyalty.

The Cuban government under Castro also clamped down on the media and restricted freedom of expression. The press was nationalized, and censorship was instituted, with the government controlling the dissemination of information and maintaining a tight hold on the narrative within the country. The government justified this control of the media as necessary to protect the revolution and prevent the spread of counter-revolutionary ideas.

Another significant aspect of repression during Castro's regime was the treatment of political dissidents. The government imprisoned a large number of people for political reasons, with human rights organizations accusing the regime of unfair trials and inhumane prison conditions. These prisoners, often labeled as "counter-revolutionaries," included political activists, journalists, and others who voiced opposition to Castro's policies.

The Cuban government's approach to opposition and dissent also extended to religious institutions and the LGBTQ+ community. The revolution's early years were marked by tensions with the Catholic Church, with the government viewing it as a bastion of counter-revolutionary sentiment. Additionally, members of the LGBTQ+ community faced persecution and discrimination, with many being sent to correctional labor camps in the 1960s and 1970s.

However, it's important to note that the level of repression in Cuba under Castro's rule has been a subject of intense debate and varying interpretations. Supporters of Castro argue that the measures taken were necessary to protect the revolution and build a socialist society in the face of internal and external threats, particularly from the United States. They point to the CIA-backed attempts to overthrow or assassinate Castro and the constant pressure from the U.S. embargo as justifications for the government's actions.

Critics, however, view the repression under Castro as a violation of human rights and an indicator of the authoritarian nature of his regime. They argue that the suppression of dissent and the lack of political pluralism in Cuba reflect a dictatorial government that prioritized control over individual freedoms.

The themes of resistance and repression are crucial aspects of Fidel Castro's biography. It highlights the challenges he faced in maintaining control and implementing his vision for Cuba and the lengths to which his government went to suppress opposition. This aspect of Castro's rule remains one of the most controversial and debated parts of his legacy, reflecting the complex and often contradictory nature of his tenure as Cuba's leader.

Chapter 7

Cuba in the Cold War

Fidel Castro's Cuba, emerging at the height of the Cold War, played a disproportionately large role in the global struggle between the East and the West. Under Castro's leadership, this small Caribbean island became a significant player in the geopolitical chess game of the 20th century, often finding itself at the center of superpower tensions.

Castro's ascent to power in 1959 coincided with intense rivalry between the United States and the Soviet Union. Initially, Castro did not openly align with either superpower. However, the radical nature of his reforms and the nationalization of American-owned properties in Cuba quickly soured relations with the United States. The U.S. responded with a trade embargo and diplomatic isolation, pushing Castro toward the Soviet Union.

The alliance between Cuba and the Soviet Union was formalized and strengthened in the early 1960s. This relationship provided Cuba with crucial economic and military support. In return, Cuba became a vital ally of the Soviet Union in the Western Hemisphere, representing a foothold for communism in America's backyard. But this alliance was not without its challenges and controversies.

One of the most dramatic episodes of the Cold War, the Cuban Missile Crisis of 1962, brought the world to the brink of nuclear war. The Soviet Union, in a strategic move to counterbalance U.S. missiles in Turkey, deployed nuclear missiles in Cuba. The United States, perceiving this as an unacceptable threat, enforced a naval blockade around Cuba, demanding the removal of the missiles. In the middle of this superpower confrontation, Castro advocated for a strong stance against the United States. The crisis was eventually defused through negotiations between the U.S. and the Soviet Union. Still, it impacted international relations and cemented Cuba's position as a significant Cold War actor.

Throughout the Cold War, Castro's Cuba actively supported anti-imperialist and socialist movements worldwide. Cuban troops were sent to various countries, most notably to Angola and Ethiopia, to support leftist governments. Castro's commitment to internationalism and his support for liberation movements in Africa and Latin America earned him both admiration and criticism. Admirers saw him as a champion of the oppressed. At the same time, critics viewed his actions as reckless interventions in the internal affairs of other nations.

Domestically, the Cold War had significant implications for Cuba. The U.S. embargo, coupled with the Soviet Union's collapse in the 1990s, plunged Cuba into economic hardship. Castro's government responded with austerity measures and a search for new financial partners. Despite these challenges, Castro maintained a firm grip on power, promoting a socialist agenda and a one-party state.

Castro's role in the Cold War also profoundly impacted Cuban society. The government's focus on national security and defense against perceived American aggression led to restrictions on civil liberties and the creation of a surveillance state. This environment contributed to a culture of political conformity and limited public dissent.

Cuba's involvement in the Cold War under Fidel Castro was multifaceted and complex. Castro navigated the treacherous waters of superpower politics, aligning with the Soviet Union and challenging U.S. hegemony in the Western Hemisphere. His actions on the international stage were bold and often controversial, reflecting his commitment to socialist principles and anti-imperialism. At home, the Cold War shaped Cuba's political, economic, and social landscape, leaving a legacy that continues to influence the country today. Castro's Cuba, small in size but large in its global impact, remains a significant chapter in the history of the Cold War.

The Cuban Missile Crisis

The Cuban Missile Crisis of October 1962 stands as one of the most critical moments in Fidel Castro's life and in the history of the Cold War. This thirteen-day standoff between the United States and the Soviet Union, with Cuba at its epicenter, brought the world perilously close to nuclear war. For Fidel Castro, this crisis tested his strategic insight and was a defining moment in Cuba's international relations.

In the early 1960s, the relationship between Cuba and the United States was already fraught following the failed Bay of Pigs invasion in 1961. Feeling threatened by the United States, Castro turned to the Soviet Union for support. Soviet Premier

Nikita Khrushchev, eager to challenge American strategic dominance, saw an opportunity in Cuba. He proposed placing nuclear missiles on the island, just 90 miles off the coast of Florida. For Castro, this offered a deterrent against further American aggression.

However, the presence of Soviet missiles in Cuba was a drastic escalation in the Cold War. When American reconnaissance planes discovered the missile sites in October 1962, President John F. Kennedy responded with a naval blockade of Cuba, demanding the removal of the missiles and the cessation of their construction.

Castro's role during the crisis was complex. He was in a precarious position, caught between two superpowers. While he had agreed to place missiles, he needed to control the situation entirely. The crisis was managed mainly by the Soviet Union and the United States, with Cuba as a vital but secondary player.

During the tense days of the crisis, Castro advocated for a strong stance against the United States. He was prepared to face the consequences, even if it meant a nuclear conflict. However, Castro's approach was not merely driven by bravado but also a calculated move to assert Cuba's sovereignty and his revolutionary credentials.

The crisis reached its peak when a U.S. U-2 spy plane was shot down over Cuba, leading to the death of the pilot. Castro had approved the deployment of Soviet-operated anti-aircraft batteries on the island, which heightened the tensions.

Awareness of the potential for global nuclear war, Kennedy and Khrushchev engaged in intense negotiations to resolve the crisis.

The resolution came when Khrushchev agreed to dismantle the missile sites in exchange for a U.S. commitment not to invade Cuba and the secret removal of American missiles from Turkey. The crisis was averted, but the resolution left Castro feeling betrayed by the Soviet Union, as he was not consulted about the final agreement.

The Cuban Missile Crisis had several significant repercussions for Castro. Firstly, it solidified Cuba's position as a critical player in the Cold War. Secondly, it assured the survival of Castro's regime by securing a promise from the United States not to invade Cuba. However, it also showed the limits of Cuba's power, as major decisions were made by the Soviet Union and the United States without Castro's direct involvement.

The crisis also profoundly impacted Castro's domestic policies and international standing. Domestically, it reinforced the need for a strong military and a centralized government to defend against external threats. Internationally, it increased Cuba's stature among socialist and non-aligned nations, with Castro being seen as a leader who stood up to American imperialism.

The Cuban Missile Crisis was a pivotal moment in Fidel Castro's leadership. It highlighted the challenges of being a small country caught in the crosshairs of superpower rivalry. The crisis tested Castro's resolve and strategic thinking and shaped Cuba's foreign and domestic policies in the subsequent years. It remains one of the most significant episodes in Castro's biography, encapsulating the high-stakes nature of global politics during the Cold War.

Aftermath and International Relations

In the aftermath of the Cuban Revolution, Fidel Castro's Cuba embarked on a tumultuous journey in international relations, navigating the complex waters of Cold War politics and beyond. Castro's foreign policy was characterized by a unique blend of defiance, strategic alliances, and a commitment to revolutionary ideals, which left a lasting impact on global dynamics.

Following the triumph of the Cuban Revolution in 1959, Cuba's international relations entered a new era. Initially, the United States recognized Castro's government, but relations quickly deteriorated due to Castro's radical socio-economic reforms, including the nationalization of U.S.-owned properties. The U.S. responded with economic sanctions and diplomatic isolation, a stance that would define its relationship with Cuba for decades to come.

Castro, in response, turned to the Soviet Union, aligning Cuba with the Eastern Bloc. This alignment was strategic and ideological, as Castro's government adopted Marxist-Leninist principles. The Soviet-Cuban alliance was cemented during the Cuban Missile Crisis of 1962, which marked the peak of Cold War tensions. The crisis also showcased Castro's role as a significant player in global politics despite leading a small island nation.

The resolution of the Cuban Missile Crisis led to a period of relative stability in Cuba's international relations. The Soviet Union became Cuba's leading economic and military supporter, providing substantial aid and assistance. This support was crucial for Cuba's survival in the face of the U.S. embargo. It allowed Castro to maintain his regime and implement his vision for a socialist society.

In the 1970s and 1980s, Castro's Cuba actively supported liberation movements and revolutionary governments worldwide, particularly in Africa and Latin America. Cuban troops were sent to countries like Angola and Ethiopia, reflecting Castro's commitment to internationalism and anti-imperialism. These interventions earned Castro both admiration and criticism: admiration from those who saw him as a champion of the oppressed and criticism from those who viewed his actions as unwarranted interference in other nations' affairs.

The collapse of the Soviet Union in 1991 had profound implications for Cuba. The loss of its primary economic and political ally plunged Cuba into a severe financial crisis known as the "Special Period." Castro's government was forced to adapt to this new reality. Despite the hardships, Castro did not abandon his socialist principles; instead, he introduced limited economic reforms to stabilize the economy while maintaining tight political control.

In the post-Cold War era, Castro sought to diversify Cuba's international relations. He cultivated ties with emerging powers and strengthened Cuba's role in the Non-Aligned Movement. Cuba's medical diplomacy, characterized by sending doctors and medical staff to various countries, bolstered its international image and created new avenues for soft power.

Relations with the United States remained strained, although there were moments of partial rapprochement, such as during the Obama administration. However, the core issues of the embargo and political differences continued to impede the full normalization of relations.

The aftermath of the Cuban Revolution and Castro's rule saw Cuba play an outsized role in international relations. Castro navigated global politics with a mix of strategic alliances, a commitment to revolutionary ideals, and a defiance of Western hegemony. His foreign policy decisions had significant implications not only for Cuba but also for the broader international community. The legacy of Castro's international relations is a complex tapestry reflective of the challenges and contradictions of leading a small nation during intense global rivalry and change.

Chapter 8

Surviving the Embargo

The story of Fidel Castro and Cuba's survival of the U.S. embargo is a tale of resilience, adaptability, and defiance. Imposed in the early 1960s, the blockade aimed to isolate Cuba economically and politically. It became a defining feature of Castro's leadership and Cuba's post-revolutionary identity, shaping the nation's economy and its place in the world.

When the embargo was first instituted, its impact was immediate and profound. Cuba, heavily reliant on trade with the United States, found its primary export and import markets abruptly closed. This economic stranglehold was designed to cripple Castro's socialist government. Still, it also galvanized the Cuban leadership's resolve to find alternatives and resist American pressure.

One of Castro's first responses was strengthening ties with the Soviet Union. This alliance provided a lifeline, as the Soviets offered economic assistance, military support, and a market for Cuban exports, primarily sugar. This support was crucial during the initial decades of the embargo, allowing Cuba to maintain its socialist programs, such as universal healthcare and education. However, this relationship also meant that Cuba's economy was tied to the fortunes of the Soviet Union, a vulnerability that would become starkly apparent with the USSR's collapse in the early 1990s.

The dissolution of the Soviet Union plunged Cuba into a severe economic crisis known as the "Special Period." After losing its primary trading partner and aid provider, Cuba faced food shortages, fuel, and basic necessities. The Special Period was a time of hardship and improvisation. Castro's government responded with economic adjustments, including limited market reforms and increased tourism and biotechnology investment emphasis. These changes, however, did not signify a wholesale shift to capitalism but rather a pragmatic approach to ensure the survival of the socialist state.

During these challenging times, Castro's charisma and ability to rally the Cuban people played a pivotal role. He framed the embargo as a battle between David and Goliath. This narrative resonated deeply with the Cuban populace and with supporters worldwide. Rather than weakening Castro's position, the embargo often reinforced his image as a nationalist hero standing up to American imperialism.

In addition to economic strategies, Cuba's embargo survival involved a significant diplomatic component. Castro actively sought to build relationships with countries across the globe, particularly those in Latin America, Africa, and the Non-Aligned Movement. These relationships were economic, political, and ideological. Cuba supported various liberation movements and provided assistance through programs like sending medical professionals abroad.

Despite these efforts, the embargo's impact on Cuba was undeniable. It hindered economic development, limited access to technology and markets, and contributed to the country's financial hardships. The Cuban government consistently blamed many of its problems on the embargo. This claim has some merit but is also a convenient tool to deflect criticism of domestic policy failures.

Over the years, international opinion has often been critical of the embargo. Many countries and international organizations, including the United Nations, have repeatedly called for its end, citing its humanitarian impact and questioning its effectiveness in achieving its stated goals.

Surviving the embargo has been a central theme in Castro's Cuba. It has shaped the island's economic policies, foreign relations, and national psyche. The embargo, intended to isolate and weaken Castro's regime, instead became a catalyst for resilience and adaptation. While it undoubtedly contributed to Cuba's economic challenges, it also played a role in forging the country's unique path in the world under Castro's leadership. The story of surviving the embargo is not just about economic survival; it's also about maintaining sovereignty and national pride in the face of immense external pressure.

Diplomacy and Espionage

In the complex tapestry of Fidel Castro's rule over Cuba, diplomacy and espionage are woven with intricate and often secretive stitches. These aspects were pivotal in shaping Cuba's foreign policy and crucial in its survival and contentious relationship with global powers, particularly the United States.

From the onset of his leadership, Castro recognized the importance of diplomacy in asserting Cuba's sovereignty and promoting its socialist ideology. However, his approach to international relations was anything but conventional. He embraced a form of diplomacy that was openly defiant of the West, especially the United States, while simultaneously building alliances that would bolster Cuba's position on the global stage.

One of the most striking features of Castro's diplomacy was his commitment to supporting liberation movements worldwide. He provided moral and sometimes material, support to various revolutionary groups in Latin America, Africa, and beyond. This policy, often perceived as meddling by the West, was integral to Castro's vision of global solidarity against imperialism and capitalism.

Castro's alliance with the Soviet Union during the Cold War significantly influenced his diplomatic efforts. Cuba became an essential ally to the Soviet bloc, serving as a strategic base in the Western Hemisphere. This relationship, however, was a double-edged sword. While it provided Cuba with necessary economic and military support, it also made the island a focal point in the superpower rivalry, most notably during the Cuban Missile Crisis of 1962.

Beyond state-level diplomacy, espionage played a crucial and often shadowy role in Castro's Cuba. Faced with the constant threat of invasion and assassination attempts, Castro's government developed an extensive intelligence network. Cuban intelligence, known for its effectiveness, played a crucial role in safeguarding the regime. It infiltrated anti-Castro groups, foiled plots against the Cuban leader, and gathered vital information about U.S. activities.

The Cuban intelligence services were not limited to defensive operations. They conducted operations abroad, gathering information from within the United States and other countries perceived as hostile to the Cuban regime. This intelligence was essential for Castro to navigate the treacherous waters of international politics and to make informed decisions about his domestic and foreign policies.

Moreover, Cuba's espionage efforts were deeply intertwined with its diplomatic initiatives. Cuban spies often operated under diplomatic cover, using embassies as bases for gathering intelligence. This espionage was a critical tool in countering American influence in Latin America and monitoring the activities of Cuban exiles and dissidents abroad.

However, these espionage activities often led to diplomatic crises. The most notable incident was the shooting down of two planes belonging to Brothers to the Rescue, a Cuban exile group, by Cuban fighter jets in 1996. This act severely strained relations with the United States and led to tightening the U.S. embargo.

Diplomacy and espionage were vital to Fidel Castro's rule. His approach to international relations was unorthodox, characterized by a blend of open defiance, strategic alliances, and covert operations. Through his diplomatic efforts, Castro positioned Cuba as a significant player in global politics, defying the odds against a backdrop of superpower rivalry and economic hardship. Simultaneously, his investment in espionage played a critical role in safeguarding his regime and furthering his strategic interests. These aspects of Castro's leadership reveal a leader who was not only a charismatic revolutionary but also a wise and pragmatic player on the world stage.

Economic Struggles and Adaptations

The economic narrative of Fidel Castro's Cuba is a saga of resilience under extreme pressures, marked by profound struggles and significant adaptations. Castro's approach to managing Cuba's economy was shaped by ideological commitment, geopolitical realities, and the relentless hostility of the United States, manifesting in a prolonged embargo that severely restricted Cuba's economic options.

When Castro came to power in 1959, he inherited an economy deeply entangled with American interests and heavily reliant on sugar exports. His early reforms included land redistribution and nationalizing foreign-owned businesses, particularly those owned by Americans. These moves, intended to reduce inequality and assert national sovereignty, had immediate and far-reaching consequences. The United States responded with an embargo, severely impacting Cuba's economy and setting the stage for the island's future economic hardships.

One of the most critical aspects of Castro's economic policy was his reliance on the Soviet Union. This alliance provided

Cuba with a safety net through trade agreements, subsidies, and financial aid. The Soviet support allowed Castro to maintain his socialist programs, including universal healthcare and education. However, this dependence also meant that Cuba's economy was inextricably linked to the fortunes of the Soviet bloc. When the Soviet Union collapsed in 1991, Cuba was plunged into a severe economic crisis known as the "Special Period."

The Special Period was characterized by fuel shortages, power outages, and scarcity of essential goods, including food. The Cuban government was forced to adapt rapidly. Castro's response combined short-term emergency measures with longer-term economic adjustments. The government introduced limited market reforms, legalized the use of the U.S. dollar, opened up to foreign investment, particularly in tourism, and encouraged the development of biotechnology and pharmaceutical industries.

Another significant adaptation was the promotion of organic farming and urban agriculture. Faced with a shortage of fuel and fertilizers, Cuba turned to low-tech, sustainable farming methods. This shift helped alleviate food shortages and positioned Cuba as a pioneer in organic farming.

Despite these adaptations, the Cuban economy struggled under the weight of the U.S. embargo, which hindered access to markets, technology, and finance. The embargo's impact was multifaceted, affecting everything from the availability of consumer goods to the state of infrastructure and the broader development of the economy.

Throughout these economic trials, Castro's leadership was marked by a balancing act between maintaining socialist principles and implementing pragmatic changes. While he allowed specific market-oriented reforms, he resisted broader economic liberalization, wary of undermining the socialist character of the Cuban state.

Castro's economic policies and his government's adaptations in response to external pressures reflected his complex legacy. On one hand, they showcased his commitment to social welfare and Cuban sovereignty. On the other hand, they exposed the vulnerabilities and inefficiencies of an economy heavily reliant on external support and controlled by a centralized state.

Castro's Cuba's economic story is one of struggle and adaptation. It highlights the challenges a small, developing country faces in maintaining its ideological path in the face of external hostility and changing global dynamics. Castro's efforts to steer Cuba through these economic challenges were marked by a mix of ideological rigidity and pragmatic adaptation, shaping the island's economic landscape for generations.

Chapter 9

Education and Healthcare Reforms

Fidel Castro's Cuba, often caught in political controversy and ideological debates, showcased significant strides in two critical societal pillars: education and healthcare. These sectors not only embody Castro's commitment to socialist principles but also represent his enduring legacy.

Upon ascending to power, Castro viewed education as a fundamental tool for social change and nation-building. His government embarked on an ambitious project to eradicate Illiteracy and make education accessible to all Cubans, regardless of their social background.

Eradicating Illiteracy: The literacy campaign of 1961 was one of Castro's earliest and most triumphant educational reforms. Volunteers, many of them young students, were dispatched across the island to teach reading and writing. This monumental effort drastically reduced the illiteracy rate from about 25% to less than 4% within a year, transforming Cuba into one of the most literate countries in Latin America.

Universal Access to Education: Castro's government established a free and universal education system, ensuring every Cuban child had access to schooling. This initiative led to a significant increase in school enrollment rates. The curriculum focused on academic learning and emphasized political ideology to cultivate a new generation of socially conscious citizens.

Higher Education and Specialization: Higher education underwent substantial expansion. Universities proliferated, and specialized institutes were established, offering various courses. Scholarships and stipends enabled students from disadvantaged backgrounds to pursue higher education, breaking down the barriers that had previously restricted these opportunities to the elite.

In healthcare, Castro's administration implemented reforms that were regarded as groundbreaking, especially for a developing country.

Universal Healthcare System: Cuba developed a national healthcare system that provided free medical services to the entire population. This system focused on preventive care and community health, with a network of clinics and hospitals accessible to all citizens.

Training Healthcare Professionals: Cuba emphasized infrastructure and human resources. It invested heavily in medical education, resulting in a high ratio of medical professionals to the population. Cuban doctors, renowned for their skills, were often sent to other countries, especially in the developing world, to provide medical assistance.

Innovations and Research: Cuba's healthcare system also became a hub for medical research. The government invested in biotechnology and pharmaceutical research, leading to innovations in vaccines and treatments for various diseases. These achievements garnered international recognition and became a source of national pride.

Despite these successes, Castro's education and healthcare reforms were not without their challenges and criticisms.

Political Indoctrination: Critics argued that the education system, while achieving high literacy rates, also served as a tool for political indoctrination, prioritizing socialist ideology over critical thinking and academic freedom.

Resource Limitations: Despite its achievements, the healthcare system often faced shortages of medical supplies and equipment, partly due to economic hardships and the US embargo. This situation led to disparities in the quality of healthcare services.

Human Rights and Freedoms: The government's prioritization of public health and education was sometimes the government's stringent control over other aspects of Cuban life, including restrictions on freedom of expression and political dissent.

Fidel Castro's educational and healthcare reforms stand out as two of the most significant accomplishments of his tenure. They reflect a profound commitment to social welfare and equality, hallmarks of his ideological stance. However, these reforms also existed within the broader context of a political regime often criticized for its authoritarian practices. Thus, Castro's legacy in these areas remains a complex and multifaceted topic, embodying both commendable achievements and contentious debates.

Arts, Culture, and Censorship under Fidel Castro

In the tapestry of Fidel Castro's Cuba, the threads of arts and culture are both vibrant and complex, interwoven with the stark reality of censorship and ideological control. While promoting certain forms of art and culture, Castro's regime simultaneously clamped down on free expression, creating a paradoxical environment for artistic development.

Promotion of the Arts: Castro's government initially invested heavily in the arts, viewing them as a means to foster a revolutionary spirit. The establishment of institutions like the Cuban Film Institute (ICAIC) in 1959 facilitated the production of both artistically rich films and ideologically aligned with the revolution.

Support for Literacy and Education: The literacy campaigns and educational reforms of the early 1960s, while primarily focused on eradicating Illiteracy, also aimed at creating a more culturally aware society. These efforts broadened the general population's access to literature and the arts, previously the domain of the elite.

Music and Dance as Cultural Pillars: Cuban music and dance flourished under Castro and became integral to the nation's cultural identity. Genres like Son, Salsa, and

Afro-Cuban jazz received state support, reinforcing Cuba's image on the global cultural stage.

However, the flourishing of arts and culture came with strings attached - the heavy hand of state control and censorship.

Censorship and Ideological Control: The government maintained strict control over the arts, ensuring they aligned with socialist values. Artists deviating from the state's ideology are often censored or marginalized. This led to a culture of self-censorship where artists were cautious about expressing dissenting views.

Umap Camps and Repression of Artists: During the 1960s, the UMAP (Military Units to Aid Production) camps were established, where artists, writers, and other individuals deemed counterrevolutionary were sent for re-education. This period is infamously remembered for its repression of intellectual and artistic freedom.

The Padilla Affair: The 1971 Padilla affair involving the poet Heberto Padilla, who was arrested and later forced to publicly denounce himself and his peers, was a glaring example of the regime's intolerance towards artistic freedom. It led to an international outcry, significantly tarnishing Castro's image among global intellectuals.

Castro's impact on Cuban arts and culture is a tale of two narratives – one of promotion and patronage, the other of suppression and censorship.

Legacy of Cultural Development: Cuban arts and culture experienced significant development despite the restrictions. Cuban cinema gained international acclaim, and Cuban music continued to be celebrated worldwide.

Intellectual Dissent and Exile: Many artists and intellectuals, unable to freely express themselves, chose exile as their canvas for creativity. This diaspora contributed to a rich and diverse Cuban culture outside the island, often in stark contrast to the narrative promoted within Cuba.

Evolving Artistic Expression: Over time, Cuban artists have found subtle ways to navigate the complex landscape of censorship, using metaphor and allegory to express dissent. This has led to a rich, albeit veiled, tradition of critical artistic expression.

Castro's rule presented a paradox for Cuban arts and culture. On the one hand, his government's support and investment led to significant development in various cultural fields. On the other, his authoritarian approach to dissent stifled artistic freedom, leading to a culture marked as much by its creativity as by its censorship. This duality is integral to understanding Fidel Castro's legacy and the resilient spirit of Cuban arts and culture.

The Cuban Identity Under Fidel Castro's Rule

Fidel Castro's Cuba, an island nation marked by its revolutionary fervor under the rule of Castro, crafted a distinct identity woven from the threads of political ideology, culture, and the enduring spirit of its people. While anchored in a history of struggle and resistance, this identity was also shaped by Castro's vision of socialism and the unique character of Cuban society.

Revolution as Identity: From the Sierra Maestra to Havana, the revolution became the cornerstone of Cuban identity under Castro. The ethos of 'Revolución' was not merely a historical event; it was a living, breathing part of Cuban daily life, informing everything from education to the arts.

National Pride and Sovereignty: Castro's defiance against American imperialism fostered a robust national pride. This Cuba stood tall against external pressures, a small island in the shadow of a superpower, asserting its right to self-determination.

Socialist Ideals and Equality: The ideology of socialism under Castro aimed at creating an egalitarian society. While the effectiveness of these policies is debated, they undoubtedly shaped the Cuban identity, with a focus on communal values and social welfare.

Music and Dance as Cultural Pillars: Cuban music and dance, intrinsic elements of the national identity, thrived under Castro. They were expressions of joy, resistance, and the Cuban spirit, blending African rhythms with Latin beats in a vibrant cultural tapestry.

Literature and Intellectual Thought: Literature in Castro's Cuba navigated the tricky waters of creative freedom and ideological constraints. Writers like Alejo Carpentier and Nicolás Guillén explored themes of identity, history, and revolution, contributing to a rich literary tradition.

Censorship and its Impacts: While the arts flourished, they did so under the watchful eye of the state. Censorship, a reality of Castro's Cuba, often stifled artistic expression. Yet, it also led to a nuanced language of metaphor and allegory in Cuban art and literature.

Resilience and Adaptability: The Cuban people, under Castro's rule, displayed remarkable resilience and adaptability. Faced with economic hardships and political restrictions, they maintained a zest for life and a strong sense of community.

Education and Healthcare: Castro's focus on education and healthcare significantly shaped the Cuban identity. The high literacy rates and access to medical care were points of pride for Cubans, reflecting a society that valued knowledge and well-being.

Diaspora and Exile: Political and economic factors shaped The Cuban diaspora, which also shaped the Cuban identity. Exiles carried their culture, memories, and perspectives, contributing to a global Cuban presence.

Under Fidel Castro, the Cuban identity was a complex amalgam of revolutionary zeal, cultural richness, socialist aspirations, and the indomitable spirit of its people. It was an identity forged in the fires of struggle, defined by its resilience in the face of challenges, and enriched by its cultural achievements. This identity, with all its contradictions and complexities, continues to define Cuba long after Castro's era, a testament to the enduring legacy of his rule.

Chapter 10

Supporting Global Revolutions

Fidel Castro, a name synonymous with the Cuban Revolution, was not just a figure confined to the boundaries of his island nation. His vision for a global revolution aimed at combating imperialism and fostering socialism led him to extend support to various international movements and regimes, often in direct defiance of the United States and its allies. This facet of Castro's leadership underlined his commitment to a global socialist fraternity and his desire to export the ideals of the Cuban Revolution beyond its shores.

Under Castro, Cuba emerged as a beacon of support for revolutionary movements worldwide. This support was not just ideological; it often translated into tangible aid—military, financial, and logistical. From Latin America to Africa, Castro's Cuba extended its solidarity to those who, in his view, fought against colonialism, imperialism, and oppression.

Castro's commitment to Latin American solidarity was evident in his unwavering support for leftist movements in the region. In countries like Bolivia, Nicaragua, and Venezuela, Castro saw the reflection of his own revolution and provided them with substantial support. This support was a strategic maneuver in the geopolitical chess game against the United States and a genuine ideological bond rooted in a shared colonial history and a common struggle against poverty and inequality.

Castro's most significant international involvement was in Africa. His decision to send Cuban troops to Angola in 1975 was a bold statement of global solidarity. This intervention not only altered the dynamics of the Cold War in Africa but also showcased Cuba's commitment to supporting anti-colonial struggles. This was not merely a political move; for Castro, it was a moral obligation to assist those fighting for self-determination.

Castro's internationalist approach was not without its costs. The economic burden of military expeditions, the loss of Cuban lives in foreign lands, and the strain on Cuba's limited resources were significant. Moreover, this global revolutionary stance exacerbated tensions with the United States, contributing to the tightening of the embargo and the isolation of Cuba on the international stage.

While many in the global South hailed Castro as a champion of anti-imperialism, he faced criticism and controversy, both at home and abroad. The involvement in foreign conflicts was often viewed as an overextension of Cuban resources, and some accused Castro of neglecting domestic issues in favor of his internationalist agenda. Furthermore, his support for specific regimes and movements was sometimes seen as controversial, leading to debates about the ethics and effectiveness of his global revolutionary strategy.

Despite the controversies and challenges, Castro's commitment to supporting global revolutions left an indelible mark on the 20th century's political landscape. This policy was driven by a combination of ideological conviction and strategic interests, reflecting his belief in a world united against imperialism and injustice. This aspect of Castro's rule remains a key component of his legacy, embodying his vision of Cuba as a central player in the global struggle for socialism.

Fidel Castro's support for global revolutions was more than a foreign policy; it was an integral part of his identity and his government's ethos. It highlighted his belief in the interconnectedness of the world's revolutionary movements and his desire to position Cuba as a vanguard in the global fight against imperialism. This chapter of Castro's leadership, fraught with complexity and contradiction, continues to evoke strong emotions and debate, underscoring the impact of his revolutionary zeal that reached far beyond Cuba's shores.

Non-Aligned Movement Leadership

In the tapestry of Fidel Castro's political life, his involvement with the Non-Aligned Movement (NAM) stands out as a testament to his diplomatic understanding and quest for a global coalition of states independent of the bipolar world order. Castro's leadership in the NAM reflected his broader vision of a world order not dominated by the United States or the Soviet Union but one where smaller nations could assert their sovereignty and collective will.

Castro's journey with the NAM began with Cuba's active participation in the organization, founded in 1961, the same period when Cuba navigated the tumultuous waters of the Cold War. The NAM, comprising countries that chose not to align formally with either superpower, resonated with Castro's national sovereignty and anti-imperialism ideology.

The pivotal moment in Castro's NAM journey was the 1979 Havana Summit, where he assumed the chairmanship of the movement. Under his leadership, the summit culminated in the Havana Declaration, a document that vigorously championed the rights of nations to determine their own fate, free from external intervention and subversion. This was more than diplomatic rhetoric; it was a reflection of Castro's own revolutionary principles.

Castro's role in the NAM was not just about rallying against the superpowers. It was also about fostering solidarity among the developing world. He understood the complexities and the diversity of the countries within the movement. He sought to unite these disparate voices under a standard banner of progress, self-determination, and resistance against neo-colonialism.

One of the challenges Castro faced as a leader within the NAM was navigating the ideological differences among its members. Not every nation shared Castro's revolutionary fervor or his socialist ideals. Yet, his diplomatic skill lay in harmonizing these divergent views and focusing on common goals, such as economic development, peace, and the fight against inequality.

Castro's leadership in the NAM had implications beyond the movement itself. It elevated Cuba's status on the global stage, showcasing it as a country capable of leading a diverse international coalition. This period also saw Cuba engaging in numerous diplomatic and humanitarian initiatives in Asia, Africa, and Latin America, consistent with the NAM's principles.

Despite the high ideals, Castro's NAM leadership attracted criticism. Skeptics viewed it as a strategic move to garner international support against the US and to spread his socialist ideology. Nonetheless, his contribution to shaping the movement's direction and fostering a sense of unity among the member states remains an indelible part of his legacy.

Fidel Castro's tenure as a leader in the Non-Aligned Movement was a significant chapter in his long political career. It showcased his ability to transcend regional politics and play a vital role in global affairs. His leadership was marked by a commitment to the principles of non-alignment and a passionate advocacy for the rights of developing nations. While his methods and motives might have been subjects of debate, his impact on the NAM and its role in world politics is undeniable. Castro's involvement with the NAM is a testament to his vision of a world where small nations could stand together, undominated by superpowers. This vision continues to resonate in the complexities of modern international relations.

Charismatic Diplomacy

Fidel Castro, a figure synonymous with the Cuban Revolution, also carved a distinctive niche in international diplomacy. His approach to foreign relations was characterized by a unique blend of charisma and defiance. This combination shaped his interactions on the global stage and left a lasting impact on international politics.

Castro's diplomatic style was as much about his personal charisma as it was about his political strategies. His appearances at international forums, often marked by his trademark olive-green military fatigues, projected the image of a revolutionary leader unyielding to Western norms. This personal flair and his oratory skills made him a compelling figure at international gatherings.

One of Castro's most memorable diplomatic moments came in 1960, during his speech at the United Nations General Assembly in New York. In a marathon address that lasted for over four hours, Castro laid out his revolutionary agenda and critiqued the policies of the superpowers, particularly the United States. His presence at the UN was not just about the speech's content; it was a performance that showcased his ability to command global attention.

Castro's diplomatic efforts extended beyond the conventional arenas of international politics. He reached out to newly independent nations in Africa, Asia, and Latin America, offering support for their struggles against colonialism and imperialism. His trips to countries like Algeria, Chile, and Angola were not just state visits but symbolic acts of solidarity with the global South. Through these gestures, Castro positioned himself and Cuba as champions of the developing world.

Amid the Cold War, Castro's Cuba navigated a precarious path between the United States and the Soviet Union. Castro's alliance with the USSR was essential to his foreign policy. Still, he maintained a certain level of independence, ensuring that Cuban interests were not entirely subsumed by those of its powerful ally. This careful balancing act was a testament to his diplomatic skill.

Castro's involvement with the Non-Aligned Movement gave him another stage to exert his influence. His leadership in the movement was not just about aligning with other nations that sought to stay independent of the superpowers; it was also an opportunity to project Cuba's voice in global debates. Under Castro, Cuba's foreign policy was about leveraging non-alignment to amplify its diplomatic presence.

Despite his charisma, Castro's diplomatic endeavors were not without controversy. His support for revolutionary movements abroad, his close ties with the Soviet Union during the Cold War, and his stance against American influence made him a polarizing figure. Critics argued that his actions often isolated Cuba on the global stage. At the same time, supporters saw him as a David standing up to the Goliath of international imperialism.

Fidel Castro's approach to international relations was marked by charismatic leadership, strategic alliances, and a steadfast commitment to his revolutionary ideals. His diplomatic style, characterized by its boldness and defiance of conventional norms, left an indelible mark on the 20th-century geopolitical landscape. Whether admired or criticized, Castro's role in shaping global politics through his unique brand of charismatic diplomacy is undeniable. His legacy in international relations continues to be a subject of study and debate, reflecting the complexities of his character and the era he helped shape.

Chapter 11

Political Purges and Executions

Fidel Castro's rise to power in Cuba was marked not only by his charismatic leadership and bold reforms but also by a darker side characterized by political purges and executions. This aspect of Castro's rule, often shrouded in controversy, reveals his governance's complex and sometimes ruthless nature.

After the triumph of the Cuban Revolution in 1959, Castro faced the daunting task of consolidating power in a nation fraught with political strife and opposition. In this volatile climate, Castro and his associates perceived dissent not merely as a political challenge but as a threat to the survival of the revolutionary state. This perspective led to a series of political purges aimed at eliminating opposition, perceived or actual.

The most vivid examples of these purges were the trials and executions that followed the revolution. Many of these trials were held publicly in sports stadiums filled with crowds, where the accused were tried for crimes ranging from war atrocities to collaboration with the Batista regime. Critics argued these trials lacked due process and were more about showcasing the new regime's authority than delivering justice. The executions that followed, often by firing squad, sent a chilling message to Castro's opponents and critics.

Another controversial aspect of Castro's rule was the establishment of Military Units to Aid Production (UMAP). These camps, which existed from 1965 to 1968, were ostensibly created for those exempt from military service. However, they turned into internment camps for a wide range of people, including political dissidents, religious activists, and members of the LGBTQ+ community. The conditions in these camps were harsh, and they remain a blemish on Castro's human rights record.

Castro's regime also maintained control through surveillance and the suppression of dissent. The Committees for the Defense of the Revolution (CDR), established in 1960, played a crucial role. Functioning as neighborhood watch groups, the CDRs monitored anti-revolutionary activity. Still, their presence also fostered an atmosphere of fear and suspicion, stifling free expression.

The political purges and executions had a profound impact on Cuban society. They created a culture of fear that permeated every aspect of life. Many intellectuals, artists, and potential political challengers fled the country or were silenced. The repercussions of these actions were far-reaching, affecting those directly targeted and casting a shadow over the broader population.

While Castro's regime brought about significant reforms in education, healthcare, and social welfare, these achievements were marred by the repressive tactics used to maintain power. The political purges and executions remain a dark chapter in Castro's legacy, raising questions about the price of his revolutionary ideals and the methods employed to achieve them.

On the one hand, there were undeniable social reforms and a steadfast commitment to Cuban sovereignty. On the other, there was a ruthless suppression of opposition, marked by political purges and executions. This complexity defines Castro's legacy and continues to fuel debate about his role in history. The impact of these actions on Cuban society and the international community offers a sobering reminder of the complex interplay between power, ideology, and human rights.

Freedom of Speech and Dissidents

Fidel Castro's Cuba, a land of revolutionary zeal and social reforms, also presents a paradoxical narrative regarding freedom of speech and the treatment of dissidents. This aspect of Castro's rule is one of the most debated and scrutinized, painting a picture of a regime that often walked a tightrope between progress and oppression.

Castro's ascent to power was fueled by his commitment to social justice, equality, and national sovereignty. These ideals, deeply rooted in Marxist-Leninist thought, were not just political slogans but the bedrock of the Cuban Revolution. However, as Castro's government transformed these ideals into reality, it became increasingly intolerant of dissenting voices. Why? One could argue that, in Castro's view, unity was paramount in building a new socialist society, and divergent opinions were seen as threats to this unity.

The Cuban government under Castro implemented various measures that effectively curtailed freedom of speech. The media was nationalized, and independent journalism became virtually non-existent. The state-controlled all media outlets, ensuring that only the government's perspective was disseminated. Cuban artists, writers, and intellectuals found themselves in a constrained space. While the regime supported arts and literature that aligned with revolutionary ideals, works that critiqued the government or strayed from the official ideology were censored or banned.

The handling of political dissidents is perhaps the most contentious aspect of Castro's rule. Critics of the regime, including journalists, activists, and political opponents, faced harassment, arbitrary detention, and even exile. Human rights organizations have documented numerous instances of the Cuban government's repressive tactics. These include the infamous 'Black Spring' of 2003, when the government arrested and swiftly sentenced 75 dissidents in summary trials.

Internationally, Castro's Cuba was often criticized for its human rights record, particularly regarding freedom of speech and political freedoms. Despite this criticism, the Castro regime maintained its policies, prioritizing the greater good of social equality and independence from foreign influence over individual political liberties.

Castro's legacy regarding freedom of speech and the treatment of dissidents is undoubtedly complex. While his government made strides in education, healthcare, and social welfare, it also restricted individual freedoms. This dichotomy is central to understanding the Cuban Revolution and its aftermath. For Castro, the revolution's success and the welfare of the people seemed to justify the means, even if those means included silencing dissent.

The chapters on freedom of speech and dissidents in Fidel Castro's Cuba narrative are the most controversial. They force us to question the balance between collective and individual liberties, state sovereignty, and human rights. As history continues to evaluate Castro's legacy, these issues remain pivotal in understanding the intricate tapestry of Cuban society and politics.

International Criticism and Defense

Fidel Castro, a figure both venerated and vilified, is one of the 20th century's most enigmatic leaders. His tenure as Cuba's head was marked by profound controversy on the international stage, attracting both criticism and defense in almost equal measure.

Right from its inception, Castro's Cuba became a focal point of international scrutiny. His revolutionary policies, particularly the nationalization of industries and establishing a one-party state, drew sharp criticism from Western powers. The United States, having had substantial economic interests in pre-revolutionary Cuba, was particularly vocal. The Castro regime's alignment with the Soviet Union during the Cold War only exacerbated tensions, leading to numerous sanctions and attempts to isolate Cuba diplomatically.

Under Castro's regime, human rights issues were another central area of international concern. Reports of political repression, censorship, and the treatment of dissenters painted a picture of a government that prioritized control over individual freedoms. Organizations like Amnesty International and Human Rights Watch frequently highlighted the plight of political prisoners and the lack of freedom of expression in Cuba.

Despite these criticisms, Castro also had his defenders on the global stage. Many in the developing world saw him as a champion of anti-imperialism and a figure who stood up to the hegemony of the United States. His initiatives in healthcare and education, which resulted in significant improvements in the quality of life for many Cubans, were often cited as significant achievements of his government. Castro's internationalism, exemplified by his support for anti-colonial movements in Africa and Latin America, further burnished his reputation as a leader committed to global justice in many quarters.

During the Cold War, Castro's Cuba was at the heart of geopolitical tensions. The Cuban Missile Crisis of 1962 brought the world to the brink of nuclear war, and Cuba's role in this crisis was heavily scrutinized. Castro's willingness to host Soviet missiles was condemned by many as a reckless gamble. In contrast, others saw it as a necessary step to safeguard the sovereignty of a small nation against a superpower.

The international community remained deeply divided over Castro and his legacy. Some criticized his methods and the lack of political plurality in Cuba. On the other hand, some lauded his resistance against American imperialism and his efforts to create an egalitarian society.

Castro was unapologetic about his policies and the direction he took Cuba in. In his view, the achievements in social welfare and preserving Cuban sovereignty justified his government's actions. He remained defiant in the face of international criticism, arguing that the right to self-determination and the fight against external domination were paramount.

While international criticism of his policies and methods was persistent, a significant section of the global community also defended and celebrated his achievements. With its unique place in global politics, Castro's Cuba continues to provoke debate and discussion, reflecting the multifaceted nature of his legacy.

In this intricate tapestry of international perspectives, Castro remains a figure of endless fascination and controversy, embodying the perennial struggle between different visions of society and governance.

Chapter 12

Post-Soviet Challenges

In the wake of the Soviet Union's dissolution in 1991, Fidel Castro's Cuba faced profound economic and political challenges. The end of the Cold War era marked a significant shift in global dynamics. For Cuba, it meant the loss of its most important ally and benefactor. This period was a test of Castro's leadership and the resilience of the Cuban revolution.

With the disintegration of the Soviet Union, Cuba lost the economic support crucial to its survival. The subsidies and trade agreements that had propped up the Cuban economy for decades vanished almost overnight. This led to the onset of the 'Special Period,' a time of severe economic hardship for the Cuban people.

The Cuban economy, heavily reliant on Soviet imports, particularly oil, faced a sudden shortage. Industries came to a standstill, and agricultural production plummeted, leading to food scarcity. The situation was exacerbated by the ongoing U.S. embargo, which further isolated Cuba economically.

Faced with these dire circumstances, Castro's government was forced to adapt. Austerity measures were implemented, and there was a push towards' self-reliance.' The Cuban government opened up to some foreign investment and tourism, a significant shift from its earlier policies. Agriculture was decentralized, and greater emphasis was placed on organic farming and urban agriculture.

Despite the economic hardships, Castro's regime managed to maintain its commitment to social welfare. The healthcare and education systems, hallmarks of the Cuban revolution, remained largely intact. This was a testament to Castro's resolve to preserve the revolution's achievements despite overwhelming challenges.

Politically, the post-Soviet era tested Castro's leadership. The collapse of communism in Eastern Europe and the Soviet Union led to a global reassessment of socialist ideologies. Castro, however, remained steadfast in his commitment to socialism, resisting calls for political liberalization.

The Cuban government increased its control over the population during this period, justifying it as necessary to safeguard the revolution. Dissent was limited, and the government employed various methods to ensure conformity and control public discourse.

With the end of the Cold War, Cuba's role in international politics also transformed. No longer the focus of superpower rivalry, Cuba sought new allies and economic partners. Castro's government forged closer ties with left-leaning governments in Latin America, particularly with Hugo Chavez's Venezuela, which provided much-needed economic aid and oil supplies.

One notable aspect of Cuba's response to the post-Soviet challenges was its emphasis on environmental sustainability.

Facing a scarcity of resources, Cuba invested in organic farming and renewable energy. These efforts were recognized globally, and Cuba was often cited as a model for sustainable development.

The post-Soviet era in Cuba was marked by significant hardships and the resilience of the Cuban people and their leader, Fidel Castro. Despite the economic Crisis and political isolation, Castro's Cuba managed to preserve much of the revolution's gains in education and healthcare. The period was a testament to Castro's ability to navigate the most challenging circumstances.

Fidel Castro's leadership during the post-Soviet era was a complex interplay of resistance, adaptation, and survival. The challenges he faced and the responses he crafted shaped the later years of his rule and left a lasting impact on Cuba's path in the 21st century. This period, perhaps more than any other, demonstrated Castro's unwavering commitment to his ideals, even as the world changed dramatically.

It speaks to the enduring legacy of a leader who remained devoted to his vision for Cuba despite the numerous challenges and criticisms.

The "Special Period" in Cuba

The "Special Period" in Cuba refers to a time of intense economic Crisis following the collapse of the Soviet Union in the early 1990s. This phase in Cuban history is not just a story of hardship and survival but also a testament to the resilience of a nation under the prolonged leadership of Fidel Castro. The period reshaped Cuba's economic, social, and political landscape, marking a significant chapter in Castro's rule.

Imagine a country suddenly losing its primary economic support overnight. That was the reality for Cuba when the Soviet Union, its main ally and trading partner, disintegrated. The Soviet subsidies, which buoyed the Cuban economy for decades, ceased. This abrupt end thrust Cuba into an economic abyss characterized by severe food shortages, medicine, and essential commodities.

The Cuban economy, which heavily depended on the Soviet bloc for trade and aid, was paralyzed. The loss of Soviet oil imports hit particularly hard, leading to widespread power outages and fuel shortages. Industries ground to a halt, and public transport became scarce. Food rationing, already a part of life in Cuba, became even more stringent. The Cuban people faced unprecedented hardships, with reports of severe malnutrition and a decline in living standards.

Fidel Castro, known for his fiery rhetoric and steadfast socialist ideals, responded to the Crisis with a blend of pragmatism and ideological firmness. He declared the beginning of the "Special Period in Time of Peace," urging the nation to brace for hard times while maintaining the socialist principles of the revolution.

Under Castro's leadership, Cuba had to rethink its economic strategies. The government reluctantly introduced market-oriented reforms, allowed more excellent foreign investment, and promoted tourism, which became a crucial source of foreign currency. Agriculture saw a shift towards organic farming methods and urban gardens, as chemical fertilizers and pesticides, once imported from the Soviet bloc, were no longer available.

Despite the economic turmoil, the Cuban government under Castro strived to uphold its commitment to social justice. The education and healthcare systems, pillars of Castro's socialist Cuba, remarkably withstood the strains of the period. However, the societal impact was profound, with increasing inequality and a noticeable shift in the values and attitudes of the Cuban people.

Politically, the "Special Period" posed significant challenges to Castro's regime. The global decline of socialism and the economic hardships led to growing dissent within Cuba. However, Castro's government managed to maintain control, often resorting to increased repression. The tightened U.S. embargo during this period further isolated Cuba but also served as a rallying cry for national unity against external pressure.

A lesser-known aspect of the "Special Period" is Cuba's forced sustainability and environmental management innovation. The Crisis led to the development of a more sustainable agricultural sector and the promotion of alternative energy sources, making Cuba a unique case study in forced environmentalism.

The "Special Period" in Cuba is a complex and multifaceted era in Castro's Cuba. It showcased Castro's ability to navigate through severe crises while maintaining the fundamental ideals of the Cuban revolution. The period was marked by significant suffering and challenges. Still, it also witnessed remarkable resilience and adaptability, both by the Cuban government and its people.

The "Special Period" stands as a crucial phase in the history of modern Cuba, shaping its path into the 21st century. It reflects the endurance of Castro's leadership and the Cuban revolution in the face of overwhelming odds, fundamentally altering the course of the nation's economic and social trajectory.

Adapting to a Changing World

In the sweeping saga of Fidel Castro's Cuba, one chapter that stands out vividly is how the nation, under his steadfast command, navigated the turbulent waters of a rapidly changing world. As the global landscape shifted with the fall of the Soviet Union and the rise of new geopolitical realities, Castro's Cuba demonstrated a remarkable capacity for adaptation, resilience, and transformation.

The collapse of the Soviet Union in the early 1990s signaled a seismic shift in global politics. For Castro, this was more than a geopolitical event; it was a direct hit to the lifeline that had sustained the Cuban economy for decades. The resulting 'Special Period' brought Cuba to its knees economically. Faced with this dire situation, Castro's regime had to make significant strategic shifts. It moved towards diversifying its international relations, reaching out to countries in Latin America, Europe, and even Canada, as well as courting foreign investment, particularly in the tourism sector.

What is most intriguing about Castro during this period was his balancing act. He managed to steer Cuba through economic reforms without fully relinquishing the island's socialist principles. This period saw the cautious introduction of market-oriented reforms and greater openness to foreign investment. Still, Castro's government kept a tight rein, ensuring that these changes did not erode the socialist fabric of Cuban society.

This era witnessed Cuba's economy slowly adapting to the new global order. Agriculture saw a shift towards organic farming, urban agriculture became more prominent, and there was an increased focus on sustainable development. Castro's administration encouraged foreign investment in the tourism sector, which soon became a vital source of foreign exchange. However, these economic changes were not without their challenges. The opening of the economy brought disparities in income and access to resources, posing a challenge to the egalitarian ideals that Castro had long championed.

Castro's foreign policy in the post-Soviet era showcased his diplomatic acumen. Despite the odds against a small island nation, he maneuvered Cuba onto the global stage with defiance and diplomacy. He strengthened alliances with leftist governments in Latin America. He sought to position Cuba as a leader in the Non-Aligned Movement. Castro's visits to countries like Venezuela and his close relationship with Hugo Chavez exemplified this new strategic alliance.

Beyond economic and political strategies, what indeed marked this era was the resilience of the Cuban people. The hardships of the 'Special Period' brought out a spirit of innovation and endurance. Castro's government, despite economic challenges, managed to maintain its achievements in healthcare and education, sectors that had been the pride of the Cuban Revolution.

Throughout these trials, Castro's leadership was a study in contrasts. He was unyielding in his core beliefs yet pragmatic in adapting to new realities. His speeches from this period reflect a leader grappling with the complexities of maintaining a socialist state in an increasingly capitalist world.

It tells the story of a nation that faced the winds of change, not by bending completely but by adapting its stance without losing its roots. Castro's ability to navigate these changes and keep Cuba afloat amid economic crises and shifting alliances is a testament to his strategic vision and his unwavering support from many Cubans.

As the world continues to evolve, Castro's Cuba during this transformative period serves as a unique example of a nation's quest to maintain its ideology while adapting to a changing global landscape.

Chapter 13

The Transfer of Power

The power transfer in his later years emerges as a pivotal and intriguing moment. It signaled not only the end of an era but also the beginning of a new chapter in Cuba's history. This phase, marked by anticipation, uncertainty, and speculation, unfolded in a manner that reflected Castro's unique approach to leadership and governance.

As the 21st century dawned, Fidel Castro, the indomitable leader of the Cuban Revolution, was aging. The man who had survived countless assassination attempts, outlasted nine U.S. presidents, and steered his country through global upheavals was finally succumbing to the inevitable wear of time. His health, which he had managed to keep out of the public eye, became a topic of international interest. Rumors swirled about his condition, but Castro, ever the master of his own narrative, kept the world guessing.

Then, in July 2006, the unthinkable happened. Fidel Castro, for the first time since his ascent to power in 1959, temporarily relinquished his duties due to an intestinal surgery. The announcement, brief and shrouded in typical secrecy, sent ripples across Cuba and the world. It was not just a matter of politics but also a profoundly emotional moment for Cubans, many of whom had known no other leader.

Interim control was handed over to Raul Castro, Fidel's brother. Raul had long been a critical figure in the Cuban government but had always remained in Fidel's towering shadow. Raul, perceived as more pragmatic and less charismatic than his brother, faced the daunting task of leading a nation in transition. The world watched, speculating on potential policy shifts and the future of Cuba's socialist model.

In February 2008, Fidel Castro made his resignation permanent. In a letter published in the state newspaper, 'Granma,' he stated that he would not accept the positions of President of the Council of State and Commander in Chief. This announcement marked the end of nearly half a century of his formal leadership. This tenure had seen Cuba through dramatic transformations, crises, and resilience.

Under Raul Castro, Cuba witnessed subtle yet significant changes. Raul implemented economic reforms to revive Cuba's economy, allowing a greater scope for private enterprise and foreign investment, albeit within the bounds of socialist principles. He also took steps to improve relations with the United States, leading to the historic restoration of diplomatic ties in 2015. These changes were cautious and measured, reflecting Raul's style of governance, which contrasted with Fidel's more radical and charismatic approach.

Fidel Castro continued to loom large throughout this transition in the Cuban psyche. Even in retirement, he remained respectful and controversial, embodying the revolution's ideals and complexities. His writings and reflections, often published in state media, continued to influence public discourse.

The transfer of power in Cuba was not just a change of leadership but a symbolic turning of pages in Cuba's history. It highlighted the challenges of succession in a system so intrinsically linked with one man's identity. The smooth transition was a testament to the structures and ideology Fidel Castro had put in place, which outlasted his active leadership.

As Cuba moves forward, the post-Castro era raises questions about the future of the island's political and economic landscape. The transition of power from Fidel to Raul Castro was more than a mere change of guard; it was a moment of introspection for a nation defining its path in a world where old alliances were fading and new challenges were emerging.

The transfer of power in Cuba, marked by the end of Fidel Castro's direct rule and the beginning of Raul Castro's leadership, was a period of significant change, yet marked by continuity. It encapsulated the end of a defining epoch in Cuban history and the cautious inception of a new one, underlining the resilience of a nation and the enduring legacy of its longest-serving leader.

Reflections on Castro's Leadership

His nearly half-century-long leadership was a tapestry of paradoxes and complexities, painting a portrait of a man who was as revered as he was reviled. Castro's leadership was a journey through the political landscape and a reflection of the human spirit in its most unyielding form.

From the very beginning, Castro's magnetic charisma was evident. His way of speaking captivated audiences, be they large crowds or individuals in a private meeting. His speeches, marathon in length and revolutionary in tone, did not just convey ideas; they stirred emotions. How did one person command such attention and devotion? Was it his unwavering conviction or his ability to articulate the dreams and frustrations of his people? Perhaps it was both.

Castro's Cuba was a land of contrasts. On the one hand, it achieved significant strides in education and healthcare, becoming a beacon in these fields for many developing countries. On the other, it was a nation where dissent was often met with repression. The question arises: Can Castro's social welfare achievements justify the restrictions on political freedoms? This moral quandary remains at the heart of debates about his leadership.

Castro's resilience in the face of internal and external crises was remarkable. Be it the Bay of Pigs invasion or the Cuban Missile Crisis, he showed a fantastic ability to navigate through tricky waters. His leadership during these tense moments was not just about strategic understanding; it was about instilling a sense of defiance against seemingly insurmountable odds in his people.

Fidel Castro was not just a national leader but a prominent figure on the international stage. His support for liberation movements in Latin America and Africa spoke of his commitment to his ideals of internationalism. His ability to maintain relations with the Soviet Union and China amid their split displayed diplomatic dexterity. Yet, this internationalist stance also drew criticism and contributed to the economic hardships faced by Cuba due to embargoes and isolation.

Economically, Castro's leadership was a turbulent journey. The U.S. embargo, the collapse of the Soviet Union, and the internal challenges of a centralized economy tested the resolve of the Cuban people. Castro's response to these challenges was a mix of defiance and adaptation, but the economic woes continued to shadow his leadership achievements.

Castro's leadership also gave rise to a strong personality cult. Streets, buildings, and billboards across Cuba were adorned with his image, and his words were quoted like scripture. While this personality cult strengthened Castro's position at home, it often raised concerns about the concentration of power and the cult's long-term implications for Cuban society.

Reflecting on Castro's leadership, we see his legacy as a complex tapestry. For some, he was a hero, a champion of people with low incomes, and an unyielding adversary of imperialism. For others, he was a dictator who suppressed freedom and stifled dissent. His life was a saga of survival, resilience, and controversy.

When summarizing Fidel Castro's leadership, one is left with more questions than answers. Was he a visionary leader who improved the lives of his people against all odds, or was he a ruler who clung to power at the expense of democratic ideals?

The truth, perhaps, lies somewhere in between. His story reminds us of the multifaceted nature of leadership and the enduring complexities of human history.

Castro's Enduring Legacy

As the sun set on Fidel Castro's rule, it left behind a legacy enshrined in the annals of history, complex and contentious, much like the man himself. A figure of paradox, Castro's leadership spanned decades, leaving a mark on Cuba and the world that continues to evoke strong emotions and debates.

Castro's ascent to power marked a new era in Cuba. From the rugged terrain of the Sierra Maestra mountains to the streets of Havana, his journey was not just a fight against a regime but an embodiment of a struggle against imperialism and inequality. His vision of a socialist Cuba, free from the shackles of foreign dominance, resonated with many, especially those marginalized by the prevailing systems.

Under Castro, Cuba witnessed transformative social changes. His government's focus on education and healthcare was revolutionary. Literacy rates soared, and healthcare became accessible to all Cubans, achievements recognized worldwide. These strides, often cited by his supporters, painted Castro as a leader who prioritized his people's welfare.

However, Castro's rule was not without its controversies. His government was often criticized for suppressing dissent and limiting freedoms. Political opponents faced imprisonment, and many could not afford freedom of speech. This darker side of Castro's legacy raises questions about the cost of his social achievements and whether they can be justified in the face of the human rights abuses that occurred.

On the international stage, Castro was both a hero and a pariah. His support for anti-imperialist movements worldwide earned him admiration in various quarters. However, this also led to strained relations with powerful nations, most notably the United States, resulting in an economic embargo that would impact Cuba for generations.

Economically, Castro's Cuba faced significant challenges. The U.S. embargo, coupled with the collapse of the Soviet Union, plunged the island into economic hardships. Castro's response to these challenges was a mix of defiance, adaptation, and a struggle to find a financial model to sustain his socialist vision in a changing world.

Cuba, under Castro, was a unique socialist experiment. It stood as a symbol of resistance against capitalist dominance. This experiment had its successes and failures but undeniably carved out a distinct path in global politics, challenging the norms of governance and economic systems.

Castro's leadership ended and marked the closing of a significant chapter in world history. His passing left Cuba at a crossroads, grappling with maintaining his legacy while navigating an uncertain future.

For some, he remains a symbol of resistance and social justice, a leader who stood tall against imperialism. For others, he is remembered as a dictator who clung to power at the expense of democracy and human rights. His life story reminds him of the complexities of leadership and the intricate tapestry of human society.

Fidel Castro's legacy is not a tale of black and white but a spectrum of grays. His leadership was a journey of defiance, resilience, and controversy, leaving a legacy that continues to be debated and analyzed. As Cuba moves forward, the shadow of Castro's rule lingers, a testament to his indelible mark on the island nation and the world.

Chapter 14

Public Perception in Cuba

Understanding how Castro was viewed by the Cuban public is akin to navigating a labyrinth of contrasting sentiments, where the path of truth is intertwined with emotions, ideologies, and the tangible realities of daily life.

In the eyes of many Cubans, Castro was, first and foremost, the revolutionary hero. His ascent to power was not merely a political victory but the underdog's triumph against a corrupt regime. For those who felt oppressed and marginalized by Batista's dictatorship, Castro was a beacon of hope. He embodied the possibility of a fairer society, where the disparities between the wealthy and the poor would be addressed. This image of Castro as a liberator, especially in the early years, was a powerful narrative that defined his public perception.

For a significant portion of the population, Castro was the architect of modern Cuba. His reforms in education and healthcare were tangible for the average Cuban. The fact that Cuba boasted one of the highest literacy rates in Latin America and a healthcare system that was the envy of developing countries was, for many, a direct result of Castro's leadership. This aspect of his rule fostered a sense of pride and achievement among Cubans, who saw their country as a small island nation standing tall against external pressures, particularly from the United States.

For another segment of the Cuban populace, Castro's rule represented oppression and the loss of fundamental freedoms. The silencing of dissent, restriction on free speech, and political imprisonment painted a very different picture of Castro. Exiles and their families, who lost property, livelihoods, and loved ones, viewed him as a dictator whose regime had robbed them of their homeland. This side of the Cuban experience, often echoed in the narratives of the Cuban diaspora, presents a stark contrast to the image of Castro as a champion of the commoner.

Some Cubans saw Castro as a pragmatist, a leader who was willing to adapt despite his ideological leanings to ensure the survival of his regime and the Cuban state. His overtures for better relations with the West post-Soviet Union and modest economic reforms in the later years were seen as pragmatic moves that kept Cuba afloat. This view, though not as dominant, reflects a segment of the Cuban population that evaluated Castro not solely on ideological grounds but on his actions to navigate Cuba through turbulent international waters.

Public perception of Fidel Castro in Cuba is as complex as the man himself. It is a spectrum of views shaped by individual experiences, generational divides, and the country's ever-evolving political landscape. For some, he remains a revered leader, the face of the Cuban revolution, and a symbol of resistance against imperialism. For others, he is a reminder of a painful past, where political freedoms were sacrificed at the altar of social reforms.

In a country that continues to grapple with his legacy, Castro remains a figure of intrigue, respect, criticism, and debate. His impact on Cuba is indisputable; however, his methods and the consequences of his rule continue to be a subject of diverse and passionate discourse among Cubans. As Cuba moves forward, the public perception of Castro will undoubtedly continue to evolve, mirroring the island's complex history and ongoing journey into the future.

The Castro Mythos

Few figures have cultivated a mythos as enigmatic and enduring as Fidel Castro in the annals of modern history. Understanding the Castro mythos is to unravel the complexities of a revered and reviled man who shaped not just the destiny of a small Caribbean island but also left an indelible mark on global politics.

Fidel Castro's early life set the stage for his mythos. Born in 1926 to a prosperous sugar plantation owner in eastern Cuba, young Fidel was a rebellious child, displaying a penchant for challenging authority early on. Radical politics and activism marked his years at the University of Havana. This period crystallized his ideology, sowing the seeds of revolution in his mind. Even then, Castro was more than just a student or a budding lawyer; he was a symbol of defiance, a precursor to the revolutionary leader he would become.

The true genesis of the Castro mythos lies in the Sierra Maestra mountains. It was here, amidst the rugged terrain, that Castro, along with Ernesto 'Che' Guevara and other revolutionaries, waged a guerilla war against Fulgencio Batista's dictatorship. The narrative of a small band of rebels challenging a tyrannical government captured the imagination of the Cuban people and the world. Castro's bearded image, fatigues, and fiery oratory became symbolic of the revolutionary spirit. He was not just a man but a personification of rebellion against oppression.

Following his ascent to power in 1959, Castro's mythos evolved. He became the statesman, the charismatic leader of a new Cuba. His lengthy speeches, often lasting hours, were not mere political rhetoric; they were performances that enthralled his supporters and infuriated his critics. In the volatile theatre of the Cold War, Castro was the David who stood against the Goliath of American imperialism. His survival of multiple assassination attempts added a layer of invincibility to his persona. He was the leader who could not be toppled, a symbol of resistance and resilience.

However, the Castro mythos is a mosaic with shades of grey. His regime's human rights record, the suppression of dissent, and the economic hardships faced by Cubans paint a complex picture. For his detractors, Castro was a tyrant, an autocrat who stifled freedom. Yet, for his admirers, he remained a champion of social justice, a leader who stood up for the marginalized. This dichotomy is at the heart of his mythos, making him a figure of admiration and aversion.

Castro's influence extended far beyond Cuba's shores. He was a crucial figure in the Non-Aligned Movement, an advocate of anti-imperialism, and a supporter of leftist revolutions worldwide. His internationalism added a global dimension to his mythos, positioning him as a leader not just of Cuba but of a broader struggle against colonialism and inequality.

Fidel Castro's passing in 2016 did little to diminish his mythos. It has become a subject of even greater examination and debate. Like his life, his legacy is a subject of deep contention and profound admiration. In Cuba, his impact is inextricable from the nation's fabric – from politics to culture.

It is a testament to how one individual can shape history, becoming more than just a leader but a symbol that endures beyond the mortal realm. As Cuba and the world continue to grapple with his legacy, the mythos of Fidel Castro remains a pivotal chapter in the story of the 20th century. This chapter continues to evoke passion, debate, and reflection.

Revisiting the Revolutionary Ideal

In the kaleidoscope of 20th-century history, Fidel Castro is a pivotal figure whose revolutionary ideals reshaped Cuba's destiny and left an indelible imprint on world politics. To understand Castro is to dive into the depths of a complex man whose vision, at once romantic and contentious, sparked a legacy that continues to elicit both admiration and criticism.

Fidel Castro's journey to becoming a revolutionary icon began in the rural landscapes of Birán, Cuba. Castro's early life was marked by a duality of privilege and rebellion. His political consciousness blossomed in the halls of the University of Havana. Here, he was not just another student but a burgeoning ideologue driven by a genuine desire for social justice and a passion for change.

The Cuba that Castro sought to transform was a land rife with inequality, a playground for the wealthy under the Batista regime. His early attempts at rebellion, including the infamous assault on the Moncada Barracks, were met with failure, imprisonment, and exile. Yet, these setbacks only fueled his resolve. In the rugged Sierra Maestra mountains, Castro, alongside Ernesto 'Che' Guevara and others, waged a guerrilla campaign that would ultimately topple Batista's government. This David-versus-Goliath struggle wasn't just a fight for Cuba; it was a beacon for anti-imperialist movements.

The triumph of the Cuban Revolution in 1959 marked the beginning of a new era. Castro emerged as the charismatic leader of a socialist Cuba, promising to rid the nation of poverty, illiteracy, and inequality. His policies transformed the social fabric of Cuba: land reforms redistributed wealth, literacy campaigns combated ignorance, and healthcare reforms aimed to ensure the well-being of every Cuban. Under his rule, Cuba became a symbol of resistance against American hegemony, especially during the Cold War.

However, Castro's Cuba was not without its paradoxes. His government's record on human rights and political freedom has been a point of heated debate. While Castro championed social reforms, his administration was marked by the suppression of dissent, censorship, and political incarcerations.

These actions painted a picture of a regime that was revolutionary yet autocratic, progressive yet oppressive.

Beyond Cuba's shores, Castro's influence was far-reaching. He was a figurehead of the Non-Aligned Movement, advocating for a world order free from the bipolarity of the Cold War. His support for liberation movements in Latin America and Africa demonstrated his commitment to his revolutionary ideals. Castro was not just a leader but an emblem of anti-imperialism and a voice for the Global South.

Fidel Castro's death in 2016 did little to quell the debates surrounding his legacy. To some, he remains a champion of the oppressed, a figure who stood up to the might of the United States and sought a more equitable world. To others, he is a reminder of the perils of authoritarianism. This leader sacrificed freedom for the sake of his ideals.

His life was a blend of idealism and pragmatism, of humanitarian goals and political realities. The Cuba that Castro left behind is a testament to these complexities – a nation proud of its achievements in education and healthcare yet grappling with economic challenges and the legacies of political repression.

Fidel Castro's life and the revolutionary ideal he pursued are more than just a chapter in history. They study the complexity of leadership and the pursuit of a vision, often at significant cost. His story invites us to reflect on the nature of revolution, the balance between ideology and governance, and the enduring question of what it means to lead a nation through turbulent times. Castro's mythos, marked by emotional support and stern criticism, challenge us to consider the multifaceted nature of political leadership and the enduring impact of a man who sought to reshape a country and an era.

Chapter 15

Influences on Latin America

The story of Fidel Castro can only be told by considering his profound impact on Latin America. His influence stretches far beyond the shores of Cuba, echoing through the corridors of time and across the vast expanse of an entire continent. Castro's role in shaping the political landscape of Latin America is a tapestry of idealism, conflict, and an unyielding belief in the power of revolution.

Castro's ascent to power in 1959 sent shockwaves throughout Latin America. Here was a man who defied a dictator, who spoke of socialism and the plight of the underprivileged, a man who stood up to the colossal power of the United States. For many in Latin America, Castro was not just a leader but a symbol of resistance against imperialism and a beacon of hope for social justice.

Castro's Cuba became a rallying point for leftist movements across Latin America. His success inspired a generation of revolutionaries, from the guerrillas in the jungles of Colombia to the young idealists in the urban centers of Buenos Aires and Santiago. His influence was not just ideological; Castro's government actively supported these movements, providing them with training, resources, and a sanctuary.

However, Castro's support for armed struggle in Latin America was not without its controversies. His unwavering commitment to exporting the revolution often put him at odds with other leftist leaders who favored more democratic or peaceful methods. The Cuban intervention in various countries was viewed by some as an act of solidarity but by others as unwelcome interference.

Cuba under Castro also served as a model for alternative social and economic systems. Many in Latin America admired his initiatives in healthcare, education, and social welfare, offering a different path to development, distinct from the capitalist model promoted by the United States.

As the Cold War waned, so did Castro's direct influence in Latin American affairs. However, his legacy continued to shape the region. The Pink Tide of the early 21st century, a wave of leftist governments across Latin America, can be partly attributed to the groundwork laid by Castro's Cuba. Leaders like Hugo Chavez in Venezuela and Evo Morales in Bolivia drew inspiration from Castro's defiance and his social policies.

Castro's impact on Latin America is a story of dualities. To his admirers, he was a revolutionary hero who stood up for the oppressed and challenged the hegemony of the United States. To his critics, he was a polarizing figure whose actions often led to further instability in the region.

Even after his death, Castro's shadow looms large over Latin America. The debates he ignited about socialism, imperialism, and revolution continue to resonate in a region that is still grappling with questions of social justice, governance, and external influence. His life remains a testament to the power of a single individual to shape the course of history, not just within their own country but across an entire continent.

His vision for a socialist Latin America was never fully realized, but the seeds he planted grew in ways that have forever altered the political, social, and ideological landscape of the region. His legacy in Latin America is a poignant reminder of the enduring influence of ideas and the power of leadership in shaping the destiny of nations.

The Cold War and Beyond

Fidel Castro, a figure synonymous with the Cuban Revolution, was more than just a leader of a small Caribbean island. His actions and ideology during the Cold War not only had a profound impact on the geopolitical landscape of the era but also shaped international relations well into the 21st century.

In 1959, the world watched as Castro's guerrilla warfare tactics overthrew Cuban dictator Fulgencio Batista. This victory was not just a local phenomenon but a symbol of anti-imperialist struggle. Castro's ascent to power marked the beginning of an era where small nations dared to stand against superpowers.

From the onset, Castro's ideology and close ties with the Soviet Union positioned Cuba at the heart of the Cold War's ideological battle. Cuba, under Castro, became a significant concern for the United States. The Bay of Pigs Invasion in 1961, a failed attempt by the CIA to overthrow Castro, only solidified his rule and pushed Cuba closer to the Soviet bloc.

1962 witnessed the peak of the Cold War tensions with the Cuban Missile Crisis. Castro allowed the Soviets to place nuclear missiles on Cuban soil, a mere 90 miles from the U.S. coast, leading the world to the brink of nuclear war. The resolution of this crisis marked a turning point in Castro's international influence, portraying him as a bold leader unafraid to challenge global superpowers.

Castro's impact went beyond the Western Hemisphere. He supported various leftist movements and governments in Africa, Asia, and Latin America. His commitment to these global liberation movements was ideological and practical, providing military assistance in conflicts like the Angolan Civil War.

The collapse of the Soviet Union in 1991 left Cuba in a precarious position, losing its primary economic and political ally. However, Castro's leadership navigated these challenging times, known as the "Special Period." Despite severe financial hardships, he kept the Cuban regime intact, demonstrating his resilience and adaptability.

Castro remained a figure of fascination and inspiration for the left worldwide throughout his rule. His defiance against American imperialism, charismatic leadership, and commitment to socialist principles made him an enduring icon for many who sought alternatives to capitalist development models.

In the post-Cold War era, Castro's Cuba faced increasing isolation as global politics shifted. However, his influence remained, particularly in Latin America, where his legacy inspired a new generation of leftist leaders. Influenced by Castro's model, countries like Venezuela, Bolivia, and Ecuador sought to chart a similar path of socialism and anti-imperialism.

Fidel Castro's story is one of contradictions and complexities. While revered by many as a champion of the oppressed, he was also criticized for authoritarian practices and human rights violations. His role in the Cold War shaped Cuba's destiny and left an indelible mark on global politics.

Even after stepping down from power and his subsequent death, Castro's influence continues to be felt. His ideas on anti-imperialism and socialism continue to resonate, particularly in regions striving for political and economic self-determination. In a world where the echoes of the Cold War still reverberate, Castro's impact as a leader who dared to stand up to the superpowers remains a significant part of global history.

Fidel Castro's role in the Cold War and its aftermath is a tale of resilience, defiance, and enduring influence. His leadership shaped the course of Cuba's history and left an enduring legacy on the international stage. As the world reflects on the Cold War era and its aftermath, Castro's role as both a revolutionary leader and a controversial figure remains critical in understanding global politics' complexities.

A Controversial Figure in History

Fidel Castro: The name alone conjures many images, emotions, and ideologies. Few figures in modern history have polarized opinion as dramatically as the bearded revolutionary who led Cuba for nearly half a century. To some, he was a liberator, a symbol of resistance against oppression. To others, a tyrant, an oppressor of freedom. His story is not just a tale of a man but of an era, an ideology, and a struggle that resonated far beyond the shores of his tiny island nation.

Fidel Alejandro Castro Ruz grew up in a politically charged era. His early exposure to the inequities in Cuban society set the stage for his lifelong battle against inequality and imperialism. Educated in Jesuit schools and later at the University of Havana, his political activism began to take shape with his opposition to corrupt governments and U.S. influence in Cuban affairs.

The assault on the Moncada Barracks in 1953 marked Castro's first significant foray into the political arena. This failed coup landed him in prison. Here, he famously declared, "History will absolve me." This statement would become emblematic of his enduring belief in his cause and place in history.

The Cuban Revolution of 1959 was a watershed moment for Cuba and the world. Under Castro's leadership, it transformed Cuba from a playground for the wealthy and corrupt into a symbol of resistance against colonialism and capitalism. His agrarian reforms, the nationalization of industries, and the push for universal education and healthcare were radical moves that earned him both admiration and animosity.

Castro's alignment with the Soviet Union placed him at the heart of the Cold War. The Cuban Missile Crisis of 1962 brought the world to the brink of nuclear war, casting him as a central figure in the global power struggle between East and West. His support for leftist movements in Latin America and Africa and his opposition to apartheid in South Africa extended his influence and controversy beyond his nation's borders.

However, Castro's rule was also marked by significant human rights concerns. Political dissent was not tolerated. The freedom of speech and the press were severely restricted, and thousands of dissenters were imprisoned, exiled, or executed. For many, these actions irreparably tarnished his image as a champion of the oppressed.

Cuba under Castro faced enormous economic challenges. The U.S. embargo, coupled with the collapse of the Soviet Union, plunged the country into severe hardship. Yet, despite these challenges, Castro's government survived, adapting to changing global circumstances and maintaining control.

Castro's leadership remains a topic of heated debate. His commitment to education and healthcare is praised as an example of his dedication to improving the lives of his people. Yet, his economic policies and political repression paint a picture of a regime that valued control over freedom.

Fidel Castro's death in 2016 marked the end of an era. His legacy is as complex as his life. He is remembered as a revolutionary hero, a champion of socialism, a voice against imperialism, and equally as a dictator who ruled with an iron fist. His influence on global politics and his role in shaping the history of the 20th century cannot be overstated.

Fidel Castro remains one of the most controversial figures in modern history. His life and leadership encapsulate the struggle of small nations against the tides of global power. He was a man who inspired millions with his ideals of social justice and equally invoked disdain for his authoritarian rule. His story is not just the story of a man but of the aspiration for a world of equality, often caught in the crossfires of ideological and geopolitical battles. As history continues to evaluate his legacy, the figure of Fidel Castro will undoubtedly continue to be a subject of debate, research, and reflection.

Chapter 16

What Ifs of Cuban History

Few threads in the tapestry of 20th-century history are as colorful and as enigmatic as those of Fidel Castro and the Cuban Revolution. His life, marked by defiance, revolution, and an iron-willed grip on power, stirs a cauldron of 'what ifs.' These hypothetical scenarios, while speculative, offer a fascinating lens through which to view a complex historical figure and the tumultuous events he shaped and was shaped by.

Castro's first foray into armed rebellion was the ill-fated attack on the Moncada Barracks in 1953. The failure of this attack led to Castro's imprisonment, during which he famously declared, "History will absolve me." But imagine if this initial uprising had been successful. Would Castro have assumed power earlier, or would it have sparked a more immediate and possibly more brutal crackdown by Fulgencio Batista's regime? A successful attack could have radically altered the trajectory of the Cuban Revolution, potentially changing its character and ideology.

Perhaps the most chilling 'what if' of Castro's era is the Cuban Missile Crisis of 1962. This 13-day standoff brought the world to the brink of nuclear war. What if one of the many near-misses during the crisis had gone awry? The global implications are staggering to consider. The resulting conflict would likely have drastically altered the course of the Cold War, with Cuba at its epicenter. The very survival of Cuba, let alone Castro's regime, would have been in severe doubt.

The Bay of Pigs Invasion in 1961 was a pivotal moment for Castro. The failed attempt by Cuban exiles, backed by the U.S., to overthrow his government bolstered his position. It pushed Cuba closer to the Soviet Union. If the invasion had succeeded, it could have resulted in a pro-U.S. government in Cuba. This shift would have dramatically altered the geopolitical landscape of the Cold War, especially in Latin America.

The collapse of the Soviet Union in 1991 plunged Cuba into an economic crisis, marking the start of the 'Special Period.' Castro's regime, which had relied heavily on Soviet support, was suddenly left to fend for itself. Had the Soviet Union survived, Castro's Cuba might have continued its socialist path with more economic stability. This continued alliance might have also sustained global communist movements, potentially altering the course of international politics.

Throughout his tenure, Castro maintained a rigid commitment to Marxist principles, often at the expense of economic viability. What if, like China under Deng Xiaoping, Castro had embraced market-oriented reforms? This scenario posits a Cuba that could have enjoyed economic growth while retaining its socialist character, potentially providing a unique model of socialist development.

Castro's regime was notorious for its suppression of political dissent and control over the media. What if he had taken a more liberal approach, allowing greater freedom of speech and political pluralism? This could have led to a more open, vibrant Cuban society, possibly averting some human rights criticisms against his government. However, it could also have threatened the stability of his regime.

The 'what ifs' of Cuban history under Fidel Castro prompted a reexamination of his legacy and the pivotal moments that defined it. They remind us of the complex interplay of individual choices, historical forces, and chance that shapes our world. While these scenarios are purely speculative, they serve as a valuable tool for understanding the impact of Castro's decisions and their indelible mark on Cuba and the world. In pondering these alternatives, one recognizes the intricate weave of history, where paths not taken are as telling as those chosen.

Fidel's Cuba in the 21st Century

As the world entered the 21st century, Fidel Castro's Cuba remained an enigma, wrapped in the cloak of revolution and resistance. The new millennium for Castro's regime was not just a change of calendar; it marked the continuation of an era, the adaptation to changing global dynamics, and the persistence of a revolutionary ideal that had admirers and critics.

The collapse of the Soviet Union in 1991 left Cuba economically and politically isolated. Yet, depending on one's viewpoint, Castro's Cuba, resilient or stubborn, managed to endure. The 'Special Period' of the 1990s, characterized by severe economic hardship, had tested the Cuban government's and its people's resolve. However, as the 21st century dawned, Cuba began to show signs of a slow recovery. This period was marked by modest economic reforms and an increased focus on tourism and biotechnology. The question lingered: How far could Castro go in liberalizing the economy without relinquishing the socialist principles that were the foundation of his regime?

Fidel Castro's Cuba in the new century continued its diplomatic tango, balancing relationships with old allies and forging new ones. The early 2000s saw strengthening ties with leftist governments in Latin America, particularly with Venezuela under Hugo Chavez. This camaraderie offered a lifeline to Cuba's economy, primarily through oil-for-doctor exchange programs. Simultaneously, the relationship with the United States remained as complex as ever. The Bush administration maintained a hardline stance, but the winds of change were brewing on the horizon.

Internally, Cuba under Castro remained essentially unchanged in terms of political structure. The government continued suppressing dissent, maintaining tight control over the media and the public sphere. This aspect of Castro's rule drew criticism from human rights organizations worldwide. Yet, there was also a sense of social stability. Education and healthcare remained robust, the twin pillars of Castro's social policy. But was this stability just a façade hiding underlying societal discontent?

As Fidel Castro aged, the inevitability of a leadership change became a topic of speculation both within and outside of Cuba. In 2006, due to health issues, Fidel temporarily handed over power to his brother, Raul Castro. This move was a precursor to the permanent transfer of power two years later, marking the end of an era. Raul's leadership brought about more significant economic reforms, suggesting a gradual shift from Fidel's hardline policies.

Fidel Castro's death in 2016 prompted a global reflection on his legacy. His Cuba in the 21st century was a testament to his ability to withstand external pressures and maintain his vision of a socialist Cuba. However, it also highlighted the shortcomings of his regime, particularly in terms of economic freedom and human rights. The world debated: Was Fidel a revolutionary hero who stood up to imperialism or a dictator who clung to power at the expense of his people's prosperity?

Post-Fidel, Cuba faces the challenge of navigating a path that honors his legacy while addressing the pressing need for reform. The 21st century has brought new global challenges, including the COVID-19 pandemic, which has hit Cuba hard, particularly in the crucial economic sector of tourism. The Cuban government now stands at a crossroads, determining how to adapt to these changing times while staying true to the revolutionary ethos that has defined it for over half a century.

Fidel's Cuba in the 21st century is a story of survival, adaptation, and unwavering commitment to certain ideals. The Cuba Fidel left behind was markedly different from the one he inherited - socially progressive in many ways but economically struggling and politically rigid. As the world evolves rapidly,

Cuba's journey post-Fidel remains one of the most intriguing narratives in global politics. Castro's legacy is not just a tale of the past but a living, evolving story that continues to unfold.

Imagining a Post-Castro Cuba

As the sun sets on Fidel Castro's era, a new dawn beckons for Cuba. The thought of a post-Castro Cuba stirs a concoction of emotions and speculation. What will this Caribbean island, so long synonymous with its revolutionary leader, look like in the aftermath of his indelible reign? Will it cling to the ideals that Castro so fervently championed, or will it navigate toward uncharted waters?

To fathom the future, one must first acknowledge the shadows of the past. Fidel Castro's Cuba was a land of paradoxes - it boasted significant achievements in education and healthcare, even as it grappled with economic woes and political dissent. The Cuban identity, deeply intertwined with Castro's ideology, faces a crossroads. Will this identity evolve or resist change?

The post-Castro era is inevitably a time for economic introspection. Cuba, under Castro, sustained a socialist economy against the tides of global capitalism. However, economic reforms seem necessary and imperative with the changing global financial landscape and the internal pressures for better living standards. Will Cuba embrace market-oriented policies or find a unique path that balances socialism with economic pragmatism?

Politically, Cuba, after Castro, stands at the brink of potential transformation. While Raul Castro's leadership marked a period of subtle shifts, the question remains: Will Cuba move towards a more open political system? The possibility of a political restructuring, perhaps even a move towards democracy, cannot be dismissed. However, the inertia of decades of one-party rule cannot be underestimated.

Fidel Castro was a figure both revered and vilified on the global stage. A post-Castro Cuba presents an opportunity to rewrite its foreign policy script. The relationship with the United States, which is always a focal point, is particularly intriguing. Will the two neighbors turn a new leaf, or will old grievances continue to strain ties? Moreover, Cuba's role in Latin America and its alignment with global powers will be aspects to watch.

Socially, Castro's Cuba made significant strides. Preserving and improving these gains in education and healthcare will be crucial. However, social freedom, particularly freedom of expression, remains contentious. The post-Castro era could be a turning point in expanding civil liberties and fostering a more open society.

Cuban culture is vibrant and has flourished even under restrictions. In a post-Castro era, one can envisage a cultural renaissance with greater artistic freedom and global exchange. However, there's also a charm in the continuity of Cuba's unique cultural identity, rooted in its revolutionary past.

The youth of Cuba, who have only known a world under Castro's shadow, will play a pivotal role in shaping this new era. Their aspirations, dreams, and visions for Cuba's future will be instrumental in driving change. Will they uphold the revolutionary spirit or steer Cuba towards a radically different path?

Imagining a post-Castro Cuba is envisioning a land at a historical juncture filled with possibilities and uncertainties. It's about contemplating change while respecting legacy, about new voices mingling with old echoes. This Cuba, ripe with potential, stands on the cusp of its history, ready to carve out a new narrative that respects its past while boldly embracing the future. The world watches with bated breath as Cuba slowly turns the pages of its next chapter.

Source Materials

Here, we present a list of references and materials that have contributed significantly to our understanding of this iconic historical figure.

"Fidel: A Critical Portrait" by Tad Szulc

This book offers an in-depth look at Castro's life, from his early days to his ascent to power. Szulc's meticulous research and interviews with key figures in Castro's life make this biography a standout.

"My Life: A Spoken Autobiography" by Fidel Castro and Ignacio Ramonet

This autobiography, based on over 100 hours of interviews, offers Castro's perspective on events throughout his life and reign. It's a window into his thoughts and motivations.

"The Autobiography of Fidel Castro" by Norberto Fuentes

Written by a former insider, this book is a blend of fact and fiction, providing a unique narrative of Castro's life and the Cuban Revolution.

"Fidel Castro: My Life: A Spoken Autobiography" by Fidel Castro and Ignacio Ramonet

A detailed autobiography that gives insight into Castro's personal experiences and views, providing a direct line to his thoughts on various matters.

"Fidel Castro: Rebel, Liberator or Dictator?" by Jules Dubois

A critical analysis of Castro's rule, Dubois' book offers a different perspective, delving into the controversies and challenges of Castro's regime.

"Che Guevara: A Revolutionary Life" by Jon Lee Anderson

While primarily about Che Guevara, Anderson's book provides substantial context about Castro and the Cuban Revolution, essential for understanding the era and the relationship between these two figures.

"Castro's Cuba, Cuba's Fidel" by Lee Lockwood

Lockwood presents an insightful look into the Cuban Revolution and Fidel Castro's role through extensive interviews and first-hand observations.

"The Real Fidel Castro" by Leycester Coltman

Coltman, who knew Castro personally, offers a balanced and comprehensive look at Castro's life, ideology, and impact.

"Havana Nocturne: How the Mob Owned Cuba and Then Lost It to the Revolution" by T.J. English

This book sheds light on the pre-revolutionary period in Cuba, providing context for the environment that led to Castro's rise.

"Cuba: A New History" by Richard Gott

Gott's book provides a broader historical context of Cuba, from its colonization to the post-Castro era, helping readers understand the socio-political landscape that shaped Castro.

"Fidel & Che: A Revolutionary Friendship" by Simon Reid-Henry

This dual biography explores the relationship between Castro and Che Guevara, offering insights into their personal bond and their joint revolutionary endeavors.

"Fidel Castro: In His Own Words" edited by Alex Moore

A collection of speeches, interviews, and writings by Castro, providing an unfiltered look into his ideologies and policies.

"Before Fidel: The Cuba I Remember" by Francisco José Moreno

Moreno's memoir offers a view of Cuba before Castro's revolution, providing a contrast to the post-revolutionary state.
"The Double Life of Fidel Castro: My 17 Years as Personal Bodyguard to El Lider Maximo" by Juan Reinaldo Sanchez

This memoir by Castro's former bodyguard reveals a different side of the Cuban leader, based on firsthand experiences.

"Fidel Castro: A Biography" by Volker Skierka

Skierka's biography is a meticulously researched account that offers both critical analysis and understanding of Castro's complex character.

Printed in Dunstable, United Kingdom